WINNING PLAYS

TACKLING ADVERSITY
AND ACHIEVING SUCCESS
IN BUSINESS AND IN LIFE

MATT MAYBERRY

CENTER
STREET

New York   Boston   Nashville

Center Street
Hachette Book Group
1290 Avenue of the Americas
New York, NY 10104
centerstreet.com
twitter.com/centerstreet

First Edition: September 2016

Center Street is a division of Hachette Book Group, Inc.
The Center Street name and logo are trademarks of Hachette
Book Group, Inc.

The publisher is not responsible for websites (or their content) that are not owned by the publisher.

The Hachette Speakers Bureau provides a wide range of authors for speaking events. To find out more, go to www.HachetteSpeakersBureau.com or call (866) 376-6591.

Library of Congress Cataloging-in-Publication Data

Names: Mayberry, Matt, 1987- author.
Title: Winning plays : a top athlete's advice for tackling adversity and
   achieving success / Matt Mayberry.
Description: First Edition. | New York : Center Street, [2016]
Identifiers: LCCN 2016015458| ISBN 9781455568284 (hardcover) | ISBN
   9781478912699 (audio download) | ISBN 9781455568260 (ebook)
Subjects: LCSH: Mayberry, Matt, 1987- | Football players—United
   States—Biography. | Football players—United States—Conduct of life. |
   Chicago Bears (Football team)—History.
Classification: LCC GV939.M49 A3 2016 | DDC 796.332092 [B]—dc23 LC
record available at https://lccn.loc.gov/2016015458

ISBNs: 978-1-4555-6828-4 (hardcover), 978-1-4555-6826-0 (ebook)

Printed in the United States of America

RRD-C

10 9 8 7 6 5 4 3 2 1

*This book is dedicated to my three angels in heaven
who have greatly impacted my life: Grampa Dee,
Uncle Tim, and Coach Hoeppner. I don't know what
I would do without the support, love, and guidance
I received from each and every one of you.
I miss you guys so much and try to make
you proud every waking moment.*

*Grampa Dee, everything that I have learned
about becoming a man came directly from you.*

*Uncle Tim, you were the first person to believe in my
vision and dreams when I officially hung up the cleats.*

*Coach Hoeppner, you looked me in the eyes when
I was eighteen years old and told me that I would be more
successful off the field than I ever would be on the field.
Because of the impact of these words, that journey has begun.*

CONTENTS

Contents

AUTHOR'S NOTE

Some incidents, events, and dialogue are drawn from my imagination and are not to be construed as real, even though they are based on real characters, conversations, and events. Most of the names used are of real people. But I have changed the names of *some* individuals and modified identifying features of others and some places in order to preserve their anonymity. The goal in all cases was to protect these people's privacy without damaging the integrity of my story.

WINNING PLAYS

INTRODUCTION

Many of life's failures are people who did not realize how close they were to success when they gave up.

—*Thomas A. Edison*

For most people, from the time we reach the age where we can read, talk, and write, the word *failure* is regarded as negative. Starting in childhood, we get it drilled into our heads that failure is appalling and unacceptable. In sports, the only celebration is the team or individual who comes out on top. The one who wins the lead in the play is applauded, and the rest who tried out are suddenly the losers. Then you have the business world, where if you fail as an employee, you may no longer be trusted with important projects, you may get demoted, or you may even be left without a job. If you're in a leadership position, it's almost certain that you will catch negative media attention and the critics will come calling left and right.

But the most successful men and women in the world—the game changers, those who have created something far bigger than most—are also the biggest failures. *How can this be?* This is because failure isn't really a failure; it's just one effort among many to move forward, to become the best you can be. It is the journey of learning from multiple failures and turning them into success over and over again. It is a process of recognizing the gift, the benefit, the lesson learned, and using it to catapult ahead. And if I can do it, anyone can.

As a former NFL linebacker for the Chicago Bears, I have had to constantly reprogram my mind and motivate myself even in the midst of some of the most difficult times in my life. As a former drug addict, I have had to continually remember who I am. The strategies I share within these pages are the same ones I've been implementing every day for the past ten years. These strategies have helped me achieve some audacious goals as an entrepreneur, a motivational speaker, and a maximum performance strategist. Once I learned to see each failure as a gift—a blessing in disguise—things started to change.

I know what it's like to be knocked down and out, and I've learned to expect challenges because that's just the way life is. You have to expect challenges, too, in order to be prepared. However, you don't have to let the challenges or apparent failures define who you are.

"But, Matt," I can hear some say. "I'm so stressed out. I have two jobs, and I'm barely making ends meet. I can't take another failure. I'll never make it."

I hear you. I understand. We're all asking more of ourselves than perhaps at any other time in history—or so we like to think. Life is difficult and complicated. It's rough out there. Wars, economic and health crises that plague the globe, and pending planetary disasters present new, unprecedented challenges for us as human beings.

But no matter what's happening in the world, we all have

dreams. We must cling to our dreams. We want to be the hero of our own destinies, winners in the game of life. No matter who we are or what country we live in, we want opportunities for advancement, good homes, significant and satisfying careers, and great relationships. We're all the same on some level. We all have goals, and we all want to believe that we can become successful.

When failures or setbacks happen, as they inevitably will, some will simply quit. Some will blame others for misfortune and settle into mediocrity. Many will want to give up, but their dreams won't let them. Having goals and dreams is important. It can help you through the hard times, the dark days. And if you quit, it's all over.

I know both sides of this coin. I often played the victim role in high school. I had to utilize whatever strength I had left within me and find new dreams and goals. Over time I have realized that we all have a spark of greatness in us. None of us is destined to be a victim. Each time we're knocked down, we have to get back up again. It's simple but true.

I'm not a victim of my past or my circumstances. I am an incredible being—a victor—who knows that the power of a champion resides within me. I'm the dreamer who keeps on dreaming. I am recognizing my gifts and acknowledging my blessings in disguise. I continue to rack up the gifts, one failure and success at a time. And I want to show that the same can be true of you.

It's never too late to begin. If you're reading this book, then I know you're curious. Perhaps my story can help you. I'll show you how to find that deep, burning flame within yourself, and I'll explain how to rekindle your dreams and become the person you were destined to be. It is my hope that this book can serve as a beacon of hope, an inspiration, and a guide on your path of life. Once you've finished it, you'll have learned how to turn any failure into a gift, redefine your philosophy on how you view adversity, and never let hard times get the best of you again.

Chapter One

ALMOST DEAD AT SIXTEEN

You learn from the mistakes you make and from the mistakes other people make. The truth is, you don't learn from success; you learn from failure.

—George Clooney

I made it to the NFL and became a linebacker for the Chicago Bears. I reached a pinnacle of success that was even greater than I ever imagined. But before all that, at sixteen, I was almost dead. At the very least, I was a wayward youth who could have easily landed in prison. At sixteen, I was already a hard-core drug addict—and I had countless lessons to learn.

I know that many people have been in the shoes I used to wear, and many people will be in those same shoes tomorrow. They will be from all ages and walks of life. Some will move forward, and some will stay in that very dangerous place, experiencing all the darkness life has to offer. The fortunate ones will recognize the gift of failure and use their failures as stepping-stones to achieve success.

Some folks like to say that people don't change, but I'm here to tell you that no matter who you are, you *can* change. You don't have to accept your failures as a one-way ticket to nowhere. Everyone has failures. We have them every day—in school, at work, in relationships, and in striving to achieve our bigger goals in life.

Throughout this book, I'll offer you surefire ways to turn those failures into gifts and successes. But first, let me describe one of my first major failures and how I reprogrammed myself and my life. That turnaround made all the difference and helped shape me into the man I am today.

Being a drug addict in high school, I hurt many people. The truth was I simply didn't care. My personal goals consisted of getting high. I had abdicated my sense of success and self-esteem to a lower, base goal of being acknowledged by other people whom I deemed to be my most prized allies. I thought I had to hang out with certain people to be accepted. This meant associating with those who were older, more popular, and into every drug imaginable—drugs that were the products of wild, delinquent, and even criminal behavior.

I'm not talking about mischievous kids who dabbled once in a while in a nefarious world for the thrill of the forbidden. No, I'm talking about diving headlong into the extreme, out-of-control behavior that hurts people. The behavior that gets people locked away in prison. And gets people killed.

One night when I was desperate to get high, I was stressed out and wanted to still my mind immediately. The thing was, I didn't have much money, and I didn't want to pay for the coke I so desperately craved. I felt entitled and believed that I deserved to have whatever I wanted.

Charlie and Joe, two drug friends I got high with often, met me that night at a vacant parking lot. "Here's our money," said Charlie, handing me a wad of small bills. "Call Robert." He told me to call because I knew how to get in touch with the well-known drug dealer.

"You know what, guys? I'm not gonna pay." Adrenaline pumped in my veins, and I felt tough, invincible. "I'm gonna knock the guy out and take everything he's got."

Charlie and Joe looked at me like I was crazy.

"Yeah, right," scoffed Joe. "Shut up. You're not going to do that. Just make the call."

I laughed. "Okay. Watch me."

I made the call, and we were given instructions on where to go. We piled into one car and drove to a secluded park to meet Robert. He stood underneath the tall oak trees, shrouded in the shadows.

"Wait here," I told Charlie and Joe.

I got out of the car, puffed up my chest, and marched over to Robert. Without saying a word, I squared my shoulders, clenched my fist, and hit him in the face as hard as I could. He crumpled to the ground with one punch. *Piece of cake*, I thought. I reached down into his coat pockets and took all his coke, weed, and money.

Full of arrogance and self-satisfaction, I sauntered back to the car.

"Good God, Matt," said Joe. "I can't believe you did that. In one punch!"

"It was easy." I laughed like it was no big deal and divvied up their share of the money and dope.

"C'mon, let's get outta here before he wakes up," said Charlie.

"Let's go see Laura," I suggested, referring to one of our friends who got high with us.

We laughed hysterically as we drove to Laura's.

Once we got there, Joe blurted, "You won't believe what Matt did."

"He knocked out the dealer in one punch," said Charlie. "You should have seen it."

"You didn't," said Laura.

"Yes, he did," said Joe. They elaborated, going over every detail with great enthusiasm as if I were a hero.

Their admiration gave me a rush of power. I had no remorse. I was so clueless; I didn't even worry about the dealer getting even with me later on. Our drug world was tough and dangerous—people got killed for stealing drugs and money from dealers. But I had no concern for the fact that I was playing with fire.

The sad thing was that I knew deep down what I was doing. Somehow I had lost all sense of logic and discrimination. No matter who I was hurting, I simply didn't care. I wanted what I wanted. Narcotics ruled my every thought, my every action.

Something was clearly bothering me, though. I had previously created lofty goals for myself for high school, college, and sports. For my career and life. When had those goals fallen away and become irrelevant?

Fear is often the catalyst for changes both good and

bad, and I suppose fear was in there somewhere. Perhaps I was afraid of not being accepted and not being good enough to achieve my big plans in life. Somehow I had picked up this sense of entitlement. I didn't even want to try. It was probably fear of *not* achieving that made me stop pursuing my goals.

After all, how many people actually attain success in sports—a career that requires skill, discipline, talent, and sometimes even a dose of good luck? I'm sure that was bothering me. But I never considered it. Whatever was disturbing me, I pushed it aside and thought only of my next quick fix. I craved that false sense of power and ego that comes from getting high and being regarded highly by those who make their own rules and break the ones they don't like.

I was young, naïve, and misdirected. Living an unexamined life, I never noticed if I was moving forward and achieving my goals, and I never questioned whether my actions were leading me to a path of success or failure. My thinking was skewed, and my attitude sucked. I felt entitled to anything I wanted. I was reckless and didn't care about anyone or anything except getting high and partying. Every street drug I could get my hands on—marijuana, crack, cocaine, quaaludes, meth, and every hallucinogen in between—I tried. My objective was to get high and stay high. That was all I thought about. As a result, I quickly spiraled into becoming a true and committed addict. I relied on my daily high to get me through the days, and I avoided thinking about what I was doing and who I was hurting. I was up for any illegal and bold challenge. I wanted to fit in and impress my wild friends.

I had turned a dark corner. My relationships with family and friends no longer mattered to me. My grades were definitely suffering. Yet somehow I remained involved in sports despite the drugs. I had always been into sports, even in elementary school. In high school, I continued playing baseball and football. In many ways, the only fragments of self-esteem and personal achievement I had left were through sports.

I'm not sure how, but I maintained my achievements in sports. I got high, and I played high. I was relaxed on drugs and somehow continued to play well. No one seemed to notice, and I thought I was fooling everyone.

It was crazy. But this was my life, and though I was hanging on by a thread, I was still hanging on.

The stark truth was that I had clearly become a delinquent and a desperate addict. And not even my teammates were safe from me. On a Thursday in May, I went into the locker room looking for money. I stole one of my teammate's wallets and took all the cash in it. I had breached the trust of my teammates already in many ways, but I had now reached a new low.

The coach found out about the incident and called me in to see him.

Feeling cocky, I sat across the desk from him with legs sprawled in front of me. I didn't have time for this.

The coach stared at me in disbelief. A part of him knew the truth, but like my family, he didn't want to believe the worst about me even when it was looking him right in the face. "Did you steal one of your teammate's wallets?" he asked point-blank.

I ignored him and gazed out the window.

The coach had a soft-spoken voice. He was not an "in your face" kind of guy, but he was firm. "I'm going to give you one chance and one chance only to tell me the truth." He folded his hands on the desk and said nothing more.

"I don't know why I'm here," I finally said, slumping my shoulders and sinking into my chair.

"Matt, you're lying." The coach's face was pinched in pain, his brows furrowed. He shook his head. "You need to go see the dean upstairs right now." I could feel his disappointment.

I didn't realize it at the time, but the coach had wanted to help me. He gave me the opportunity to tell him the truth. But I had done everything I could to steel myself against his earnest attempt to get me through this.

I had failed a key test. The one guy who was willing to help me find my way got up and shut the door behind me as I walked out of the room. He was done with me.

I had just lost a true ally, and my future was now in my own reckless hands. I was spiraling downward even farther.

I walked upstairs to the dean's office and went in with a smug smile. There was no way I was going to admit the truth, and there was no way they could know the real truth.

The dean was a stern man and the ultimate disciplinarian. He was a "take no prisoners" sort of guy. "We got word that you stole one of your teammate's wallets. Is this true?" He folded his arms and looked at me with burning eyes.

"No, it's not true." I stared back at him, daring him to question me.

"Follow me," the dean said as he picked up his keys.

We headed downstairs to the boys' locker room. He went straight to my locker and unlocked it.

"What are you doing? You can't go through my stuff!"

Despite my protests, the dean rummaged through my personal belongings and found my backpack. There, at the bottom of the backpack, was the missing wallet. "Matt, you are in serious trouble. Not only did you steal your teammate's wallet, but you lied to all of us."

I was furious. *How dare he go through my things! He couldn't do that!*

"Follow me," said the dean.

We returned to his office, and he dealt out my punishment. "I'm going to suspend you for one day and give you five days of detention."

I looked at him blankly but laughed to myself. *Really? That's it? That's all you've got? What a joke.*

"Matt, it is a privilege to be a student athlete here at Hinsdale South, and you haven't lived up to the standards. I am forced to release you from the baseball team."

That was a direct hit to my heart. "What do you mean? You're kicking me off the baseball team? You can't take that away from me. You can't do that! I'm the best player on the team and you know it, and you're kicking me off? You guys *need* me!"

The dean picked up a ballpoint pen and tapped it on a pad of paper like a toy drum. He knew I was throwing my talent away, but he was resigned to this decision. "We can do whatever we want, and that's exactly what we're doing. You're excused. You can go now."

Baseball had always been my best sport, giving me the only true sense of confidence I had ever known. I was a standout youth, and my coaches had insisted that I had all the talent in the world. I was told repeatedly that I could get drafted professionally. Up until high school, I, too, thought that would happen.

Somewhere I had lost the dream and my confidence to achieve it. Everything completely changed when drugs became my priority. I had stopped looking toward my goals. I had lost my vision, my sense of hope, and my potential. Things took a bleak turn after I got kicked off the baseball team. My heart began to pound to the beat of defeat and failure.

I teetered on the edge of getting thrown out of school altogether. As I tested everyone, I disrespected my teachers and fought anyone who so much as looked at me the wrong way. *I, Matt Mayberry, am a force to be reckoned with, and I dare you to question me or try me.* I vandalized anything that wasn't mine, I was truant, and I was failing all my classes. I lost count of my suspensions. How I wasn't expelled entirely is still a wonder to me.

What is even more of a wonder is how my life turned around. Little did I know that the next decade would be completely altered and I would be transformed. It wasn't long ago that I was invited to be a featured guest at that same high school in Illinois where I was kicked off the baseball team. As the speaker at their staff breakfast, I gave an inspirational message and reminisced about my dark days at Hinsdale South and my journey over the past ten years to where I am now. I thanked the school for not expelling me and for giving me endless chances. Shortly afterward, they nominated me for the Hinsdale South Hall of Fame.

But in 2004, that vision of achievement was not even a remote possibility.

Back then, my guidance counselor told me that if I didn't change my life immediately, I would probably never graduate from high school and could end up in jail or be dead before my eighteenth birthday.

Their warnings had no effect on me. I scoffed at their concern and the disappointment in their eyes. I could do no wrong! I was overbearing, falsely confident, disrespectful, and driven by only one motivation—to escape reality by getting high. In that world of narcotics I felt powerful, popular, and awesome.

I don't blame anyone else for my actions. Today, I refuse to take the "victim" route. I came from a good family and a good neighborhood. My parents were happily married, churchgoing folks. I was simply my own biggest problem, yet I thought my problems were because of everyone else—not me. After all, I was invincible!

That feeling of invincibility stemmed from the high of drugs, and it made me destructive and reckless. I lived for immediate and temporary gratification and fulfillment—my next high. I searched for it in dark places. Dangerous places. The next puff of a blunt, the next swig from the whiskey bottle, the next wild party. I had no faith in anything other than drugs and myself. Everything was about *me*. And I was willing to live my life to the fullest at everyone else's expense.

When I was sixteen, during the height of this crazy era in my life, I received a letter from my grandparents, the only people I had any type of compassion for at the time. A line in the letter grabbed my attention:

"Matt, you're slowly killing all of us. Your grandma and I are dying because of you."

That letter touched a small part of my cynical, cold heart. For a few short minutes, I felt a bit of shame. In Leonard Cohen's song "Anthem," he wrote about how light can get through the cracks.

When my grandparents wrote me that letter, they opened a tiny crack, and a tiny bit of light seeped through that tiny crack into my dark world.

It can take a while to learn a life lesson, though, and once again, I catapulted into a dark, dark place.

YOUR OWN PERSONAL GAME PLAN TO PUT INTO ACTION

1. Refuse to be degraded. Don't let those closest to you degrade your potential. I wasn't born into an environment that would predict I would become a full-blown drug addict at the age of sixteen. I had a good, loving family and a nice life. No, it was because of the people I surrounded myself with on a daily basis. John C. Maxwell states in his book *How Successful People Grow*, "According to research by social psychologist Dr. David McCleland of Harvard, the people with whom you habitually associate are called your 'reference group,' and these people determine as much as 95 percent of your success or failure in life." Think about that for a minute—*95 percent*. If you're wondering if the percentage in that study is correct, that's not the point. The point is that who we choose to spend our time with absolutely makes a difference in our lives. When people express to me how disappointed they are or how big of a rut they're in, I ask them to check their inner circles. This certainly isn't the case all the time, but more often than not, a link within an inner circle has been sabotaging their success.

2. Friend analysis. Take the time right now to examine your inner circle. Are the people you associate with adding value to your life? Or are they hindering you from reaching your true potential?

- Does your daily environment force and encourage you to grow?
- Are you constantly stepping out of your comfort zone?
- Are you excited and passionate about life?
- Are you challenged to become a better man or woman?
- Does your vision for your future inspire you?
- Are you fired up, or discouraged, each time you share a new idea or dream of yours with your inner circle?
- Do you view failure as a gift and an opportunity to help you get to where you want to go?

If you answered no to more than four of the above questions, your current group of friends and inner circle may be preventing your growth and success. I'm not telling you to immediately get rid of your close friends or cut off ties with beloved family members. However, I hope you start to analyze the members of your inner circle.

3. Be authentic! Be unique! Don't try to fit in. Dare to stand out. Be you! Looking back on my journey and everything that went wrong during that dark period of my life, I wanted to fit in. I stopped being myself and thought it was cool to hang out with people who snorted cocaine and broke the law. Since then I've learned that one of the most powerful characteristics, at least in my humble opinion, is authenticity. Don't spend one minute trying to "fit in" just because you think that's the cool thing to do. Being your unique self is an extraordinary gift that the world needs. You have talents and abilities that no one else has. At the end of your life, you'll never regret living authentically and staying true to who you are. The power of authenticity in business is a game changer as well. It lets your customers, prospects, and everyone else know that you're *real*. The brands that neglect the human touch or forget that business *is* and *always will be* about people are missing a major component of what it takes to win.

Creating a list of all the characteristics and values that make up Matt Mayberry and that I want to embody has helped me stay true to who I am. My list contains five key values and then five characteristics I strive to practice and instill in my everyday life. I carry this list always. I have one version in my briefcase, another on my desktop, and a final version on my mobile phone.

Make your own list and carry it with you. It will motivate you to become the best version of yourself.

Chapter Two

DRUG REHAB: THE BIG CON

Very little is needed to make a happy life; it is all within
yourself, in your way of thinking.

—attributed to Marcus Aurelius

I didn't know exactly what it meant to go astray, to fall short,
to lose my way, when I was sixteen. Back then, I thought I
knew everything about life and that I had all the answers.

As I got halfway through my grandparents' letter, a sen-
tence captured my full attention: "Matt, if you go to the drug
treatment facility, we will give you $500."

I have always loved my grandparents more than anything,
but being in the depraved world that I was living in for so
long, I have to admit that the only thing that completely
reeled me in was the five hundred dollars. *Ka-ching!* When
they mentioned the money, I pictured all the cocaine and
weed I could purchase with it.

My grandparents had started the "intervention" conversation with this particular letter after my parents learned
that I tested positive for cocaine at my annual physical. I

had merely laughed at their attempt to enlist me in an out-patient rehabilitation facility. This was who I was. In my eyes, it was *just cocaine*. I was actually more surprised that cocaine was the only thing that showed up in my results. I was living so recklessly that cocaine in my bloodstream—one of the most destructive and addictive narcotics on the planet—received a simple shrug from me. My nonchalance terrified my family.

Everyone thought it would be best if I first heard and saw the letter from my grandparents concerning a treatment facility, but I immediately freaked out.

"Mom," I said, "what the hell are they talking about?"

Mom stood at the kitchen sink, gazing out the window. She turned around and looked at me, then said softly, "This is all that's left. You need help, and we've tried nearly everything to get you back on the right track. We simply can't do this anymore. You need to go to a treatment facility."

I scoffed at my mom. I felt empowered from a line of coke I had snorted earlier, and the familiar wave of adrenaline started to pump through me. *What does this woman know? How dare she and everyone else tell me that I need a treatment facility?*

"Please, Matt, just hear me out."

"Screw this." With the letter from my grandparents in my hand, I stomped outside. I couldn't stand being in the house with her anymore. She was stifling me. I was sixteen and six foot two. I could make my own decisions. She couldn't tell me what to do. My dad and my grandparents couldn't, either.

I paced around the yard. A couple of neighbors waved to me. I ignored them. A dog dashed across the street toward me with a ball, wanting to play. I yelled at him to get away.

Twenty minutes clicked by. I reread the letter from my grandparents. They were two of the most important people in my life. I felt that my own parents were clueless, but Grampa Dee (as we lovingly called him) and Grandma were not. Yet, more than anything—more than hearing their words of love and concern and being empathetic to their pain and worries—I selfishly focused on the five hundred dollars they promised to give me if I'd go to rehab. I envisioned buying a ton of dope, then selling it for double the cost and making a thousand bucks or more. My buddies would be impressed, and the girls would come around, knowing I had cash to spend and a stash to blow through. This was just what I needed to make me happy.

Remember how I mentioned that tiny crack of light shining through when I received the letter from my grandparents? Well, there it was again. A tiny crack of light—very tiny, I might add—snuck its way into my cold, cold heart.

The authorities at my high school were sick and tired of my criminal, arrogant behavior. It had robbed so many people of their peace of mind and happiness. And already, my guidance counselor had warned me that if I continued down the path I was currently on, I would either end up dead or in prison. But I had sneered, knowing I was too smart and too strong for that.

TACKLE THIS TODAY

Do you know how to recognize when your heart is closed off to the light? Do you know how to open that crack to let the light shine in?

But there was that tiny bit of light again. It was obvious that my parents, the two people who had brought me into this world and had given me everything possible to have a good life, were at the end of their ropes. Then there were my grandparents. They were also actively involved in my life, since they lived practically next door. They were slowly but surely deteriorating mentally and physically from the stress and chaos caused by my behavior. My drug-induced consciousness told me they were all overreacting.

I was very reluctant about the drug rehab program, but I realized I could score some brownie points with my grandparents and parents and earn five hundred dollars to boot. Plus, if it was a day treatment program, I wouldn't even have to spend the nights there. It could work. I could make everyone believe I was on the mend, and I would impress my coaches, teachers, and family. They wouldn't have a clue that I was going to use the five hundred dollars to feed my habit and hopefully double my money. *Yeah, that's the way to go*, I decided. It was the "Big Con." And I was the perfect person to pull it off.

I walked back into the house and approached my mother in the kitchen. "Okay," I said.

"What do you mean?" she asked.

I couldn't help but notice that her eyes were wet and red. It dawned on me that many afternoons, I would come home and find her with wet, red eyes. I'd just never paid much attention before.

"I'll go into the drug treatment program," I told her flatly. "I'll do it."

"You will?" Mom looked at me with total surprise and a wee bit of hope.

Although I was high at the time, I still remember my mother's expression when I told her the news.

"That's what I said."

"Oh, Matt...that's wonderful." Tears welled up in her eyes again, but I didn't want to see it.

"I don't want to hear any more about it. I said I'd go, so that's it."

Without saying another word, Mom nodded.

In the back of my mind, I knew that the last thing I wanted to do was put any energy toward getting sober, drug free, and healthy. I was determined to live my life exactly the way I wanted to, regardless of whom I hurt along the way.

THINGS YOU CAN TACKLE NOW TO OPEN UP TO THE LIGHT

1. Smile at yourself in the mirror. I know this sounds simplistic, but if you want to change your mood from angry to happy, just smile. This comes from that old adage of turning a frown upside down that our teachers talked about when we were in school. And it really does work. It's almost impossible to stay angry at yourself or anyone else if you stop and smile. And when you smile, the "light" enters into your world.

2. Focus on someone you love. Even at my angriest, when I thought about my grandparents—people I loved with all my heart—a tiny crack of light peered through the darkness. So today, practice focusing on someone who loves you or whom you love, and embrace that feeling.

3. Surrender your feelings of unworthiness. Many times, those angry feelings stem from not feeling worthy of success or happiness. When you feel "less than," you can act out or become resistant to any good thoughts or encouragement from anyone. Surrender those nasty feelings, and you'll be amazed at the difference in the way you feel.

You can't redirect where you are headed or change yourself if you personally don't want that for your life. It's a choice. I couldn't become healthy and work toward creating a better future if I didn't want to do what was necessary to make that a reality.

My parents, my grandparents, and all the people who loved me couldn't change my life unless I wanted to. It was up to me. Sure, our friends and family can offer their support, provide us with resources, and be there every step of the way. But if we don't want to become better and we don't do the necessary work, at the end of the day none of that really matters. It's a very sad truth, but that's why so many men and women have such unhappy and unfulfilled lives. They have completely neglected what's most important, which is taking full responsibility for themselves. When you stop playing the "blame game," pointing the finger, and making excuses for why you haven't experienced success or happiness, that's when things really begin to transform.

And at sixteen, I didn't want to change. I wanted to continue on my path with reckless abandon. Without a care in the world, I lived every single day high, ruining the lives of so many.

TACKLE THIS TODAY

Are you used to playing the "blame game" when you've done something wrong? Do you take responsibility for your actions?

My parents nearly had to wrestle me into the car every day to get me to rehab. It was their unwavering commitment and unconditional love that made all the difference.

My first day at the treatment facility was miserable. From the moment I walked in, I hated everything about it and wanted absolutely nothing to do with being there. But I knew the only way I was going to receive the five hundred dollars from my grandparents was to show up and appear interested. It was an act, of course. A "Big Con."

As I sat in a group session among the addicts, my mind drifted. *I'm not one of them. I'm not an addict.* I was totally in charge of myself. I fantasized about the fun things I could be doing instead of sitting here with a bunch of losers.

As each minute ticked by, I felt more and more miserable and started to hate everything and everyone around me. I thought about how great it would be to get high.

I pictured all the people I would rather be spending my time with, the friends I got high with, the group I partied with. All I had to do was give them a call, and someone would come and get me.

The people at the treatment facility depressed me. I couldn't stand them. The therapists and doctors had just met me, but they kept telling me that I was living my life the wrong way. I could barely stand the sound of their voices. *They're idiots. Losers. Who chooses to do this for a living, anyway? What can they possibly know about a sixteen-year-old who plays sports and is popular?* I had a fantastic life. The best!

Several weeks into my drug treatment program, I came home for dinner one night. Gary, my thirteen-year-old brother, and my mother and father were waiting for me with one of Mom's special dishes, homemade spaghetti, simmering on the stove, ready to be devoured. Generally, I'd be ravenous to sit down and eat a heaping plateful of my mom's special recipe. Even though the food smelled delicious, I had something else on my mind.

My family looked at me eagerly—hopefully—as I sat down at the table. They desperately wanted to know I was getting the help I needed so I could return to my old self—the Matt before the drugs.

As rude as ever, I wore headphones and listened to music. Normally, my parents wouldn't have allowed the headphones at the dinner table, but they didn't say anything because I was in such a fragile state. They were afraid to set me off.

Mom and Dad were happy that I was in the rehab program, and they walked on eggshells, trying not to incite any sort of relapse or rebellion from me.

When my family tried to engage me in conversation, I stared at my food and paid no attention to them. All I could think about was getting high and contacting my friends. When you come off drugs after being dependent on them for so long, your emotions fall to an all-time low. The highs are so high and so fulfilling, but the lows take you even lower. That's the cycle of addiction. You begin to crave a constant high. There's a continual need. A nagging dependence on the instantaneous escape and thrill, the adrenaline and the false sense of happiness that substance abuse provides. I was drug free for two weeks, the longest I had ever been without getting high, and I felt the lowest low and craved the highest high more than I ever had in the past. I couldn't stomach the idea of returning to that drug treatment facility. Those people made me sick.

I vaguely heard Mom and Dad suggest things they could do to help me get back on track. My younger brother even piped up and mentioned that he'd love to go out and pitch a few baseballs. He was into sports the way I always had been. They were frantically trying to unlock my stubbornness.

As dinner was nearing the end, my father excused himself. "It's been a long day, and if you guys don't mind, I'm going upstairs to my room."

Mom nodded. "I'll be up after I take care of the dishes." She turned to Gary. "Will you help me clear the table?"

"Sure, Mom," he said.

I kept my eyes glued to the table. I avoided looking at them.

Shortly after, while Mom and Gary were clearing the table, I followed Dad's lead, and, without saying "excuse me" or anything else, I headed upstairs to take a shower.

As I got midway up the stairs, my father said in a quiet, gentle voice, "C'mere, Matt." It was a voice I had never heard from him before. For a second, it sent chills down my spine. It was foreboding. Of what, I didn't know.

I was not in the mood to talk. I was still agitated and pissed off that I had agreed to go to the drug treatment facility in the first place. "Whaddya want?"

The strongest man I have ever come face-to-face with has not been a three-hundred-pound offensive lineman in college or the NFL. No. It's my father. He *was*—and *still is*—one of the strongest human beings I have ever met. He has been an ironworker for the past thirty-plus years, exemplifying what a blue-collar work ethic is through and through. He has always lived a very simple but meaningful life.

I headed to my parents' room. I had to get this over with. As soon as I stepped inside, I could see that his eyes were watery. I suspected he was going to tell me something that had been weighing on his heart for quite some time.

"Son, your mother and I love you with all our heart," Dad said, "but we don't know if we can go on anymore living like this. We worry about you from the time we wake up until the moment we go to bed. It's not healthy, and slowly but surely, we're running out of ideas and options. We love you and are willing to do whatever it takes to help you get back on track, but we're just lost and confused."

I gave him a blank look.

"Is it something that we did as parents along the way?" Dad asked. He then questioned the way he and Mom raised me.

Truth be told, I have the best parents in the world. My mother and father are the true definition of phenomenal caregivers who love their children with an extraordinary amount of unconditional love.

My state of being had nothing to do with what my mom and dad did as parents. It was *everything* that I had done as a teen. It was the people I hung out with and my attitude. It was feeling sorry for myself and focusing on everything that was *wrong with myself and my life*. I had so many things to be positive about and grateful for, but I didn't recognize any of them. For me, the only positive was the fact that I had drug buddies to hang out with. That I knew where to buy drugs for the "low." That I was powerful.

It wasn't my parents; it was all me. Even though I heard my father loud and clear and actually felt bad for him for a fraction of a second—remember, now and then a tiny bit of light would get in—I still let what he said go in one ear and out the other.

"Can I go now?" I sneered, ignoring his plea.

"Go, just go." He knew it was useless. He knew I didn't want to hear anything he had to say. That I was beyond listening.

My father's words forced me to look back at my life, and I entered a very dark place. An ominous place. I started to see demons, but what I was really seeing was *myself*. I saw a scumbag of a person who caused more turmoil and heartache in people's lives than most people ever will. I felt like a complete disgrace. A ferocious rage and anger burned inside me that I had never felt before. The anger ate me up, and I spiraled out of control.

Barreling toward my bedroom, I punched the walls in the hallway. I had put many holes in my parents' walls over the years. I needed to numb my mind, so I ripped out the drawers in my chest and dresser, flinging out the clothes, searching for the coke I'd hidden in my socks. *Nothing? What the hell? I had to find something! Where's that weed?* I flipped over my mattress, tearing off the sheets and bedspread. I was a madman, a maniac, tearing through shelves and boxes and destroying my room.

TACKLE THIS TODAY

Can you recall one time that you became so angry that you wanted to punch anything and everyone around you? How did you handle this anger?

Sweat streamed down my forehead and into my eyes, burning them. I wiped my eyes with my sleeve and cursed silently. I couldn't find any goddamn thing anywhere. Of course, my parents had searched my room and removed all the drugs I had strategically hidden, and they'd thrown them in the dumpster two weeks ago when I entered rehab. *I should have hidden them in my brother's sock drawer. They wouldn't have searched there.* I cursed them under my breath for invading my privacy. For stealing my belongings. My happiness. For denying me this pleasure.

I was so furious that I couldn't get the quick fix I was yearning for that I did a face-plant on my bed and then, like a deranged boxer, took full swings at my pillows, punching the hell out of them, to release the anger that was boiling inside me.

What happened next completely transformed my dark, depraved world and set my life on a whole new course forever.

YOUR OWN PERSONAL GAME PLAN TO PUT INTO ACTION

1. Go within. Real, lasting change starts from within. You can't alter the outcome of your life unless you first decide to change yourself as a person. I didn't want to change when I first went to the drug rehab facility. I hated everything about it and only went because of the five hundred dollars my grandparents told me they'd give me if I worked hard and got myself clean. But honestly, if you want something different for your life and you want to change for the better, then you have to do the "inner work" to affect the "outer circumstances." Money, fame, a great job—none of that will transform you permanently if you don't do the work on yourself. Just as addicts can't change their lives and get clean unless they truly want to, the same applies for anyone who desires a different life. Tools you can use to change your inner self include prayer, meditation, studying, and practicing. Surrendering yourself to a higher power can also help manifest the change you want in your life.

2. You are your own master. When I couldn't find drugs that evening in my room, I freaked out. I wasn't in charge of my emotions, my destiny, my thoughts, or my life. The drugs ruled me. They were my master. You may not be a former drug addict like me. Have you thought about changing your actions and thoughts so you can change your life? What can you do to truly become the master of your own life?

3. Your mind can be your ally. Allow your mind to work *for* you, not against you. When I was in the shower the night of my unsuccessful search for drugs, I let my mind work against me. I believed my world was a complete disaster and that my life sucked. We are in control of what we think about and what we feed into our minds on a daily basis. Start viewing your mind as the grand master of your life, the ruler of your destiny, because that's exactly what it is. I highly suggest *As a Man Thinketh* by James Allen. It's a classic book on the power of your mind and thoughts. And it's a very valuable tool to help you learn how to be the master of your life.

Chapter Three

IN PURSUIT OF MY DREAMS

Darkness cannot drive out darkness; only light can do that.
Hate cannot drive out hate; only love can do that.

—*Martin Luther King Jr.*

It surprised me when it happened. But I have learned that sometimes mercy and grace can enter our lives so effortlessly, so completely that it can take our breath away. And we are forever changed. Just like that.

After completely freaking out over the conversation with my father and then failing to find my stash still in the house, I collected myself and headed into the bathroom for a much-needed shower.

The hot water sprayed on my face and beaded on my shoulders, then trailed down my arms and swirled into the drain on the floor. I blinked hard as I contemplated the conversation with my father. I didn't know what to think, but to be completely honest, a tiny part of me was aware of the extreme hurt and pain that I had inflicted on my loved ones.

At the same time, a demon raised its ugly head, and *that part of me* was thoroughly pissed off that I couldn't find the drugs I had hidden so carefully. It was particularly furious about the invasion of my privacy that robbed me of my fix in my most desperate of times. I never needed a high like I did then. The sobriety had me at an all-time low. This was an unfamiliar place for me. I desperately wanted to revel in the comfort of an adrenaline rush. I wanted to feel alive again. That invincible bubble of happiness.

That "good" part of me argued with the demon and couldn't believe that I had been sober for three weeks. For the past couple of years, there wasn't a day that had passed when I wasn't high on something.

After I finished up in the shower, I returned to my room. All of a sudden, I felt an urge to stop right where I was and look in the mirror. In three years, I had not *really* looked. How many times had my mother and father, my grandparents, my teachers, and my coaches begged me, "Matt, take a good look at yourself in the mirror." Thousands and thousands of times.

TACKLE THIS TODAY

Stop what you're doing and take a good look at yourself in the mirror. What do you see? Do you like the person looking back at you? If not, what would you like to change?

I gathered up the strength and courage to look at myself in the mirror. Staring back at me was an arrogant sixteen-year-old who thought he was an adult. Dark hair, chiseled jawline, broad shoulders. I felt no love—only hatred—for this teenager. I saw a monster, a demon, a devil. I saw anger, confusion, and depression. And I saw all the tears and turmoil that I had inflicted on so many people—especially the ones who had put their lives on hold just for me.

I didn't necessarily believe in epiphanies or moments that had the power to completely change one's life in an instant. Not until then.

Sometimes when I'm onstage describing what happened, my eyes well up because I can still feel the emotion and power of that moment. When I decided to finally look at myself in the mirror.

The flood of emotions felt like several three-hundred-pound offensive linemen were running straight at me, determined to crush me. I couldn't breathe. The years of bottled-up rage, derailed dreams in my best sport, failures in my classes, unsuccessful drug rehabilitation, the pain I had caused everyone around me, and the hatred I had for myself all collided like the veins of a lightning bolt in the sky, and it struck the core of my being.

I collapsed on my knees and cried out to God, "Help me! God, please help me!"

I grew up in a devout Catholic family who instilled spirituality in me at a young age, but during that part of my life, I didn't believe in a higher power—in God—or anything bigger than myself. In fact, I had thought I *was* God. If anything else, drugs were my God. I listened to no one but myself. I didn't abide by the law. I stole things, robbed and conned people. And I laughed and bragged about it. The worst—the very worst—was that I hurt the people who loved me most as I went out of my way to live a soulless, reckless, and wicked life.

For the first time in a long while, I was able to see myself and my situation clearly. And I hated the ugly monster that had looked back at me in the mirror.

With tears streaming down my face, I kept repeating, "God, I know I have been a terrible, terrible person the last couple of years, but what can I do to get myself out of this miserable world that I have created for myself? How can I repay my parents and grandparents and everyone else for all the pain I've caused? Please show me the way out of this mess, God."

And just like that, it happened. My answer. I wasn't necessarily expecting some sort of miracle, but after sobbing hard for fifteen minutes and having a deep, intimate conversation with God for the first time in five years, I heard the word *athletics* over and over again. *Athletics? Yes, athletics.*

I realized that maybe—just maybe—I could turn my biggest failure of becoming a delinquent teenage addict into something better. Feeling the light seep into my cold, dark soul, I had a glimmer of understanding that failure could be turned into a gift of the most divine kind when one has faith in something bigger than himself.

I had already been kicked off the baseball team, but I still had football. Though I was passionate about football, it wasn't a sport I was naturally good at, like baseball.

In the blink of an eye, with my eyes blurry and my mouth salty with tears, I knew that the only way to get myself completely out of this bleak and depressing world I had created for myself was to get a college scholarship. Maybe then I could heal the hearts of the ones who loved me. Maybe then I could heal my own sorry soul.

I honestly didn't know how it was going to happen. One thing for sure was that I had a bad reputation at my high school. I lacked the resources, stats, and support to get a scholarship. But I was already at rock bottom. I had nothing to lose.

In that moment I truly discovered the power of setting goals—of having a dream—and what can happen when you simply ask, "What can I do to change my life?"

TACKLE THIS TODAY

Have you established any new goals today that can change your life?

When you possess an unwavering belief or dream about something that tugs at your heart and you passionately want to fight for that dream, then you have a beginning, a nugget of raw clay that you can shape and mold.

My father used to leave inspirational books around the house, hoping I'd stumble across one and read it. That evening, after my shower and talk with God, I picked up *See You at the Top* by the legendary Zig Ziglar. When I looked inside the book, I noticed the chapter about goal setting was dog-eared. It focused on the importance of goals in all areas of our lives.

While I wanted to change my entire life completely, the

main goal at that point—the *game-changing goal,* as I called it—was to get a Division I college scholarship for football.

I took the index cards on my nightstand that were supposed to be used for an upcoming math test. I wrote on one side of a card, "I will receive a Division I college scholarship for football by next year."

On the flip side of the card, I wrote down two inspirational quotes by Zig Ziglar that really touched my heart.

1. "You don't have to be great to start, but you have to start to be great."
2. "You were designed for accomplishment, engineered for success, and endowed with the seeds of greatness."*

I still have this index card. When I wrote my goal on it, I didn't know what I was doing. But after my epiphany, I wanted to achieve something worthwhile. I wanted to be successful. I needed to find ways to motivate myself when frustration, confusion, or a lack of confidence interfered.

I strongly believe in the power of visualization. We must "see that image" in our mind before we ever venture forth to manifest it.

Jim Carrey is one of my favorite examples of this. The famous comedian and actor was once a "wannabe." I remember seeing a highlight of his appearance on *The Oprah Winfrey Show* back in 1997, and he spoke about his early days trying to make it in the entertainment business. He was broke and had no future. But he took a blank check and wrote out ten

---

* Quotes Archives, www.ziglar.com/category/quotes.

million dollars to himself for acting services rendered and dated it for Thanksgiving 1995.

He said that he carried that check in his wallet at all times and looked at it every morning, visualizing receiving ten million dollars. Five years after he wrote the check to himself and right before Thanksgiving 1995, he found out that he was going to make ten million dollars from the movie *Dumb and Dumber*. That's the power of visualizing your dreams. That's the power of dreaming. That's the power of relentlessly believing and working toward your vision every single day.

TACKLE THIS TODAY

What have you visualized today that you would like to see come to fruition? Make your own list of things you would like to accomplish and put it in your wallet. Look at it every day and visualize your dreams.

In the same way, I looked at my index card every day and visualized receiving a Division I college scholarship for football. I was determined to do all that I could to make it happen.

THINGS YOU CAN TACKLE NOW TO VISUALIZE YOUR DREAMS

1. Visualization. If you can't see it, then it's not going to happen. In order to achieve your biggest goals and dreams, you have to picture yourself victorious. You have to look beyond your current circumstances and past failures. Visualize as many details as you can. If you're on the beach, feel the warm sun on your body, the wind in your hair, the salty ocean waves spraying on your face. Imagine the environment, the people around you, what you're wearing, what you're hearing. Re-create any feelings that are in alignment with your dreams. For me, I visualized myself playing college football. I smelled the locker room and the cut grass on the football field, and I heard the crowds in the bleachers as they shouted for Matt Mayberry.

If you make this part of your daily routine, you will be amazed at the improvement in your life and astounded when your dream is realized.

2. Index cards. From my 3 × 5 index cards, I read daily: "I will receive a Division I college scholarship for football by next year." I could feel how awesome the moment was, and I felt happy and alive. Get in the habit of doing this every day as I did. Each morning and each night, read those index cards, close your eyes, and imagine yourself accomplishing and following through on those goals.

3. Vision boards. A vision board worked wonders in my life when I believed there was no bigger future in store for me. It gave me the chance to actually see my goals. This vision board can be a poster board, a piece of paper, the back of a cardboard box, or anything you have. You could even use a vision book. On the vision board or inside the book, put pictures that illustrate what you desire in your life. For me, it was photos of college football players who played their optimal best. I wanted to be one of the best, too. On my vision board I also posted quotes that embodied what I wanted, and I read them every single day.

4. Happy, loving memories. It's important to constantly feed your mind with happy, loving memories. I'm not referring to reliving the past, but to re-creating those moments that once made you smile. Recall times of happiness in your home, such as a birthday party, a get-together with friends, a special holiday, or something encouraging a loved one expressed. Do whatever you have to do to keep the naysayers and negative people out of your life as much as possible. You need all the happiness and love you can surround yourself with if you want to constantly focus and work toward your dreams.

I'll never forget how ecstatic I was when I finally returned to school after completing the drug program. I looked forward to telling everyone, including old and new friends, coaches, and teachers, about my new goal.

The first person I told was Kevin, a former teammate on the baseball team. Kevin started to laugh and almost burst into tears from laughing so hard.

Sure, the majority of the school knew that I had been a hard-core drug addict and was in and out of school often, but I was still stunned and hurt that he didn't take me seriously.

Kevin stopped laughing when he noticed my blank look. "You aren't serious, are you? I mean, uh, dude, face it. You have no chance of getting a scholarship. Everyone knows that. I'm sorry to deliver the bad news, but you're out of your mind. Are you still high or something? Is this the coke talking?"

"Um, no," I said. But honestly, what did I expect? I was the same kid who had been cutting class and getting high just weeks ago. I was the same kid who had been kicked off the baseball team, and now I wanted to get a Division I scholarship to some of the biggest football programs in the country. I was delusional. A complete joke.

Kevin wasn't the only one to question my ambitious and lofty new goal. I still remember how many people doubted me, saying I would never amount to anything.

Surprisingly, I changed my perspective and attitude. Instead of getting mad at the naysayers, I used all the self-doubt and negativity to fuel my strength to prove them wrong. I was already lower than low, and I was out of options. This was it for me, and I was damned if I would let anyone get between me and my end goal. I didn't care that almost everyone—even some of my closest friends since childhood—doubted me and laughed in my face.

That night when I returned home after my first day back at school, I ran upstairs and made a list of everything I had to do to receive a college scholarship for football. I carried that to-do list with me along with my index cards.

I understood why I had landed in a treatment center, and I had to figure out how to avoid this kind of thing again. I had to *analyze* and *understand* why I had done what I did with the drugs and how to move forward. First and foremost, I had to stop going out, nix all the partying, and get rid of the old crew I used to hang out with.

I remembered how my father had always told me how

important reading was. If I wanted to stay positive while embarking on this major challenge, I not only needed to grow up and develop as a strong young adult, but I also had to constantly feed my mind with uplifting material. This would guide me through the hurdles and roadblocks that I would definitely encounter on my journey.

Reading numerous motivational, thought-leadership, and inspirational books helped me immensely, and I still read as many of those by my favorite authors as I can. The books shed new light on my issues and provided a road map for me on my own educational and professional quests.

Next, I knew I had to improve physically and get faster on the football field. As a recovering teenage drug addict, I had to perform extraordinarily and do something that would astound the scouts. I wanted to catch the eye of college football coaches everywhere around the country.

Even as a baseball player, I remembered the old saying "Speed kills." For some odd reason, I took that saying with me every day when I left the house and used it as my mantra. In every gym session and every practice, I said over and over: "Speed kills."

Many times while I was on my quest to get a Division I college scholarship, I recalled happy childhood memories of playing baseball and football with Dad and Grampa Dee. It was my very favorite thing to do. On Saturdays, Grampa Dee, Dad, and I would go to the park across the street from our house and throw baseballs or footballs. After playing ball, Grampa Dee would sit with me on the grass, leaning back against an old oak tree, and say, "Matt, you are very special, and I know you're going to grow up to be great."

A thing like that sticks in a child's mind. I honestly believe it helped shape the man I am today, and I will always be grateful for Grampa Dee's faith in me. Even now when I think of how I treated him during my drug-addiction days, I cringe.

So while I worked to achieve my goal of getting a Division I college scholarship, I reflected often on happy memories of playing sports with Dad and Grampa Dee. I also reflected on running after my father in the summer when he coached junior football. I was a little kid at the time, barely big enough to lug a baseball bat around, but those memories made me very, very happy. All these cheerful, loving thoughts kept the door wide open for the light to pour through, and as the light poured through, I powered through on my journey.

My parents were a tremendous help when I shared my goal. At first they didn't have a clue how to support me, but they asked around, and, without thinking twice, they made even more sacrifices. First, they hired a speed coach; next, a strength coach; and third, a mental game coach. They did everything they could to help me achieve my dreams. Despite my troubled past, my parents' belief in me never wavered.

Lastly, I knew that if this major goal was going to become a reality, I needed to be relentless, focused, and persistent. I had to constantly take massive action every minute of every day. Success rarely, if ever, just comes knocking on your door. It takes a ridiculous amount of work, persistence, and focused action day after day, month after month, and year after year.

Many people sit around and wait for opportunities to come to them. They wait for the right people to enter their life. They wait for the perfect moment to start trying to achieve their dreams. They wait and wait for years, and soon, before you know it, they're on their deathbed, wondering what happened to all those dreams and goals.

There is no such thing as a perfect time to begin working toward building the life of your dreams or relentlessly pursuing your passion. I used to be a huge fan of the saying "Follow your passion," but then I realized that following your passion isn't enough. You need to not only follow your passion, but you need to aggressively work and persistently fight for your passion every single day.

As for my drug buddies, they remained the same. It was hard for them to believe I didn't want to party anymore.

Joe was one of the first to approach me. "Hey, Matt, glad you're out. I know you're dying to smoke a bowl," he said with a smirk.

"Nah," I said. "I'm clean."

"Ah, c'mon now," Joe said. "I know you can't resist some grass. Or how about some X? C'mon, dude, I got some new shit for you. Come to Laura's and get high with us. The gang's all there. We've missed you."

I thought about all those supposedly good "friends" whom I once spent my days getting high with. I had no desire to go back to that old life. "I told you I'm clean."

Joe shrugged. "Well, when you change your mind—"

"I won't," I interrupted him.

"Oh, you're too good for us now? You go to the psych ward and think you're too good?" He laughed.

Referring to rehab as the psych ward got under my skin. I ignored his instigation and turned to walk away, feeling a glare behind me. He was pissed, but he also knew not to incite me further. He knew what I once did to those who tried me. I never saw Joe again.

My mission to land a Division I scholarship in exactly one year was in full effect. I searched the Internet to learn how to achieve this dream. I read about football coaches and what they looked for and athletes who had excelled. Every moment of every day, I did something that would take my game to the next level and put me in a position to win.

To get rid of that failure mind-set I had adopted when I was an addict, I needed to *expand* myself to stand out physically, mentally, and emotionally. Increasing my actions, positive thoughts, and belief in myself was a way to *increase* everything in my world.

TACKLE THIS TODAY

What are you doing today to expand your own world? How do your positive thoughts and actions contribute to building the kind of world you dream about?

Whether it was studying with tutors to get my grades back on track, going to Speed School with notable speed coach Tim Graf, improving my physical strength with my trainer, Dave Johnson, or working on my mental game with Marc Anderson, I did everything possible to make my dream come true. I was determined to prove everyone wrong who doubted me.

I didn't care if I was overtraining at the time, as plenty of people thought. I wanted this more than I had ever wanted anything in my life. I was willing to work out for two to three hours each day, seven days a week.

Moving from one coach to the next, I took my index card and read it before each workout, each training session. I looked down at my card and recited the words multiple times with deep conviction: "Without a doubt, I will receive a Division I scholarship." This mantra became a part of me, and as time went on, I truly started to believe it with all my heart.

My parents took me to college camps during the weekends at universities all over the country. Then they'd drive me all the way back to Chicago on Sunday, just in time for school on Monday. Talk about dedication. My parents were the true MVPs of my life.

While researching what it took to get a scholarship and the attention of college coaches, I learned about the Nike Football Training Camps on college campuses throughout the United States. They attract coaches from nearly every college, and they're similar to the camps for the NFL, except they're for high school players instead of professionals. The attendees get tested on how fast they run, how high they jump, and how strong they are, and then they break off into different groups to perform actual football drills.

I learned that the closest camp was in Michigan, but my father suggested going to the one at the University of Georgia in Athens. I looked at him like he was crazy.

"Look, Matt, if you're really serious about this, then you need to surround yourself with the best athletes and football players in the country and *beat* them. And they're the best in the South. You should think about attending the camp in Georgia."

I considered it for a moment. I had family in Auburn, Alabama, and my father went to college at Auburn, so I was aware of how serious they were about football in the South. These athletes and coaches would be tough. It was a much different mind-set than in the Midwest. It was a religion. Football in the South is a way of life. "Okay, if you think this is the best, I'll go to the Nike Training Camp in Athens, Georgia."

If you want to be the best, you must beat the best. Everyone wants to be great and reach achievement milestones, but not everyone is willing to commit to the grueling process that it takes to be great. Many people give up after one try, after one failure. They settle for *average* instead of *great*.

The one thing I wanted more than anything was greatness, and absolutely nothing was going to stop me. I didn't always know what my next step should be or how things would turn out, but I knew that I was never going to be stagnant.

It turned out my father and I had a wonderful time at the camp in Athens. It was such a rewarding experience to see some of the best coaches in the country up close and personal, then to realize how far I'd come. I had escaped that drug-induced world and was now an athlete who was going after his dream. With my father beside me, it was an incredible moment. One I'll never forget.

At the camp, I had a phenomenal outing, running fast, jumping high, and displaying my strength. The months and months of hard work in the weight room, along with the support from my parents and coaches, enabled me to perform in the top tier for running backs. I was overjoyed! My dad was overjoyed!

From the moment I left that camp, the coaches started calling, the letters began pouring in, and my life changed. My first scholarship offer came from Northwestern University, right in my hometown of Chicago.

After the offer from Northwestern, it was like a domino effect. Other schools that had seen me perform at the Nike camp aggressively recruited me.

The second school to offer me a scholarship caught my attention right from the beginning. Indiana University wasn't the best football school, but it had just hired a new head coach. Terry Hoeppner hailed from Miami University in Ohio, having coached the Miami RedHawks from 1999 to 2004, and he had a great track record. After being hired as head coach in 2004, Hoeppner nicknamed the Hoosiers' home field "the Rock" and had a giant limestone boulder added to Memorial Stadium to reinforce the message. The coach also introduced a game-day ritual called "the Walk," in which fans and players paraded to the stadium through a parking lot full of tailgaters. I had tremendous respect for Coach Hoeppner.

As the scholarship offers continued, all the people who once doubted me tried to become my best friends. They looked me straight in the eye and professed how they'd always believed in me. When some heaped glory and attention on me, I couldn't help but laugh. It pushed me even further in the right direction, because I knew I must be doing something right.

With over a dozen scholarship offers from Division I schools, spanning the Big Ten, the Big 12, the Atlantic Coast Conference (ACC), and the Pac-12 conferences, I was torn as to which university to choose. Northwestern and Indiana grabbed my interest, because they were the first two schools willing to take a chance on me—and that meant the world to me, but I really didn't have any favorites at the time. The process became even more difficult when everyone hurled their opinions at me.

I had to stop and reflect on the roller coaster my high school journey had been thus far—being kicked off the baseball team and watching my Major League Baseball dreams diminish, entering rehab, and working sunup to sundown to earn a college scholarship. Although I believed I would obtain a college scholarship, I never imagined I would be sitting there choosing which offer I wanted from nineteen possibilities! The feeling was surreal.

This was all before my senior year in high school. I had played a phenomenal junior year of football and was getting close to one of the biggest decisions of my life. After discussions with my family and support system, I decided to choose the offer before the start of my senior season. Then I could get it out of the way and give a university an oral commitment, allowing me to give my team everything I had and go all out for my final season as a high school football player. Which I did. Since the buzz from colleges spread all over, I was invited to announce my decision on local TV, and I agreed.

During a tough few weeks leading up to the big night, a

lot of things started to weigh on my heart. *What if I make the wrong decision? Or what if it's not the most popular decision?*

After months of going through the recruiting process, I knew in my heart that Indiana University was the place for me. Many of my friends and the outside world would be shocked if I picked a mediocre football school over other universities that were notoriously good at football year after year. But the men who won me over were Head Coach Terry Hoeppner and Assistant Head Coach Bill Lynch. They assured me that if I came to Indiana, not only would I become a great football player, but I would become a better man. Even more important than becoming a great football player, the coaches promised me that I would one day go on to become more successful outside of football than I ever was at playing the game. I needed that reassurance. I needed that expectation to keep me on track when I went off to college. My parents wouldn't be there to help me anymore.

That night, in front of hundreds of people packed into a high school gymnasium, I pulled a cream-and-crimson Indiana University hat out of my duffel bag. I smiled from ear to ear as I put the hat on and the audience clapped and cheered for me. My heart swelled so big, I thought it would burst.

This was the beginning of creating a whole new legacy after I had slowly rebuilt the trust, love, and faith in all the people whom I had hurt so deeply with my delinquent behavior for so many years.

I went on to be the team captain my senior season. I had already accepted my Division I scholarship offer, so I was ready to show off for my future college team. I rushed for

2,242 yards and 36 touchdowns while guiding the Hinsdale South Hornets to a 10-2 finish my senior year. I received All-State honors as well as the Suburban Life All-Area Football Player of the Year award. I graduated having broken six school records for career rushing yards (2,827), career touchdowns (39), single-season rushing yards (2,242), touchdowns in a single season (36), points in a single season (186), and touchdowns in a single game (5).

When you stay focused on your dream in spite of the naysayers, when you lose yourself in something *bigger* than your little mind and diligently work for a cause greater than money, fame, or recognition, that's where the birth of miracles takes place.

YOUR OWN PERSONAL GAME PLAN TO PUT INTO ACTION

1. Rebuild. Have you been torn down after a particular failure? Have you wondered how you would reboot and rebuild your life? You can't sit around and wait for a miracle to just fall into your lap. You have to take charge of the situation and look for guidance to start the rebuilding process. When I had my epiphany and collapsed to my knees, I didn't ask God for a miracle. Instead, I asked Him to help point me in the right direction and show me how to get myself out of that mess. I think it's human nature to want the quickest and easiest way of getting through a difficult time. But the real "gift" lies in moving toward another direction. Whatever difficulty you're facing, search for a turnoff road and another direction to take your first step toward creating a new, bigger future.

2. The power of goals. Some people don't know how to set goals, and they certainly don't know how to go about achieving them. Nothing has changed my life more than learning how to set goals and then working hard to attain them. I have learned there is a major difference between *goal setting* and *goal achieving*. Both are important, but setting goals alone isn't enough. If you write down a goal on a piece of paper, then put that paper away in a folder and never do anything about it, you've wasted your time. You have to take action to achieve your goals. Everywhere I go to speak in the world, I share this exact same goal-setting process that has shaped my life year after year. My process has helped me to achieve every major goal that I ever set for myself. Start by setting a stopwatch or the timer on your phone for two to three minutes. This is to force you to write down your goals quickly. You can't dawdle. The reason is to eliminate the tendency to start worrying. When we consider the goals we want to achieve, we immediately start thinking about reasons why we can't reach those goals. There will be roadblocks, lack of money, and a million and one other things. If you set a stopwatch for two to three minutes, that short time span will force you to focus and write down what's really in your heart instead of wasting time on challenges down the road. The next part of the process is to write down eight to ten goals you want to achieve this time next year. It's good to include some balance on that list with health, fitness, family, leisure, financial, and business goals, to name a few. Then circle the one goal that has the potential to completely change the course of your life and serve as a domino effect for every other goal on the list. This is what I call the game-changer goal. One of mine was to get that Division I college scholarship. I knew if I achieved that major goal, it would help me reach every other goal on my list and drastically change my life.

What about you? Circle your game-changer goal, then write down twenty to fifty things you need to do to achieve it. This puts you in the small percentage of high achievers and significantly increases your odds of success. Goal setting has completely changed my life, and it can do the same for you.

Chapter Four

COACH HEP

I have learned that success is to be measured not so much by the position that one has reached in life as by the obstacles which he has had to overcome while trying to succeed.

—*Booker T. Washington*

No one expects tragedies to happen. Especially during college. Those things happen to other people, not us. When tragedies do occur—and they will whether we like it or not—it can take a while for the memories to soften and not be so painful. It can take a while to find the courage to go on with our lives.

More than likely, we all have something stored in our memory banks that has haunted us or hurt us deeply. Maybe it's something we've done—like me with my drug years—but it can also be something that was caused by someone we love or by something we wish we could have done differently. Hopefully, as we age we become wiser. If we hadn't gone through those experiences—the failures, the mistakes, the heartaches, the tragedies—we might not have grown into the people we are today.

I still get asked if I regret my decision to take a scholarship at Indiana University in Bloomington when I had the opportunity to go to highly acclaimed football schools with unbelievable winning traditions. Everywhere I travel to speak to groups and organizations, this question is brought up at least five times after my presentation while I'm chatting with the attendees offstage. My response every single time is, "Absolutely not. I have no regrets at all going to Indiana University. As a matter of fact, it ended up becoming a major blessing in my life that changed me as a man forever."

It may sound like a clichéd response, but I truly mean that statement. There are many reasons why Indiana University transformed me, but one of the main ones was Coach Terry Hoeppner. Almost everything I know about leadership stems from Coach Hoeppner—a leader, coach, mentor, father, husband, and friend.

Titles don't define leadership, and titles don't define who a man is. A certain title may have others calling you their boss, but true leadership is much more than just a label. It involves the imagining and execution of a grand vision, where leaders enroll others to be passionate about effectuating that vision and bringing it to reality.

Coach "Hep" not only had the players on board, but the entire Indiana community as a whole. Indiana has always been a predominantly basketball state, so to have the community recognize and champion football the way it did when I was there is a true testament to Coach Hep. His humility, positive energy, and willingness and ability to lead by example are what made him such a phenomenal trailblazer at Indiana.

KEY LEADERSHIP TRAITS OF EVERY GREAT LEADER

While thinking about Coach Hep, I realized there are three traits that he and all effective leaders share.

1. **They possess a deep sense of humility.**

   The best coaches I ever had in football were also the coaches who were the most humble. They were always thinking about those they were leading and rarely about themselves. In my life as a public speaker, I see the same trait in the high-performing and dominant organizations that I spend time with. The one key characteristic that all the top executives possess is humility. Top employees never want to work for, or be associated with, leaders who are arrogant and egocentric. As Billy Graham once said, "The smallest package in the world is a man all wrapped up in himself."*

2. **They radiate positive energy.**

   Just like in life, the business world is full of sudden twists, turns, and obstacles, but the most effective leaders never let the unexpected destroy their positive energy. It's your job as a leader to stay positive and strong in the face of uncertainty. Your people already have enough demands at work and at home. Don't sabotage your employees' or your organization's growth by putting negative energy into the workplace. As the

---

* Bob Proctor, *The ABCs of Success: The Essential Principles from America's Greatest Prosperity Teacher* (New York: Jeremy P. Tarcher / Penguin, 2015).

leader, you set the tone. Whether that tone is positive or negative is completely up to you. If you're not radiating positive energy, how do you expect your people to?

3. **They lead by example.**

This one may seem self-explanatory, but you would be shocked at the number of leaders who would never consider doing what they ask of those they lead. One of the best ways to lose the respect and trust of your people is to continually fail to lead by example. Look at any phenomenal leader. For example, take Bono, the lead singer of U2. When interviewed by Misty Meeks in *Fortune* magazine, he said, "Real leadership is when everyone else feels in charge."* True to his word, Bono has always made everyone else feel important when it comes to giving back to life. According to the article, Bono's accomplishments are exemplary. Not only did he help persuade global leaders to write off debt owed by the poorest countries, but he also encouraged political administrations and others to vastly increase AIDS relief. He continually serves mankind by enlisting major companies and millions of people worldwide to combat AIDS, poverty, and preventable diseases.

Moreover, leaders are self-starters. They live what they preach. They demand excellence from themselves first before they ever demand excellence from anyone else. That was Coach Hep to a tee.

---

* Quoted in Misty Meeks, "Fortune Magazine's 50 Greatest Leaders," *Texture by Next Issue*, April 1, 2014. https://www.texture.ca/en/2014/04/01/fortune-magazines-50-greatest-leaders.

I'll never forget my first official visit to Indiana University. I was already quite sure I wanted to go to Indiana, but it was a tradition to visit the ones that were interested in you before you made up your mind.

On this visit, I was invited to Coach Hep's house to meet with him and his wife, Jane. I was nervous. I admired the man so much and wanted him to like me and be assured that I would do everything I could to be the best football player on the field.

I remember arriving at his house promptly at 1:00 P.M. It was a warm day with a cloudless sky. Coach Hep's home was situated in a comfortable suburb in Bloomington, complete with dogs running in the yards and children riding bicycles down the sidewalks.

My hands felt sweaty, and my heart beat faster than normal. I took a deep breath and rang the doorbell.

Within a couple of minutes, he opened it. "Matt Mayberry! Nice to meet you, young man," he said, smiling at me. I immediately felt at home.

We shook hands, and he invited me to follow him to the den. He then introduced me to his wife.

"Matt, would you like some coffee or tea? Or maybe a bottle of water?" Jane asked.

"Coffee would be great," I told her.

After she brought two mugs of coffee, Coach Hep and I sat together, discussing how wonderful Indiana University was. He didn't beat around the bush. He leaned forward and looked directly into my eyes. "Do you want to be a part of something special?"

I knew right then and there that Indiana was the school

for me. I wanted to be a part of something special, regardless of what others thought.

But before I could respond, he continued, "Of course, you can go to a program that has been great for decades and maybe contribute extensively your junior year, or you can come to Indiana and contribute right away and become one of the main focal points in building a great football program."

"It sounds great," I told him. "I'd love to help build a great football program."

That day Coach Hep said something else that still resonates in my heart. "Well, come to Indiana and you *will excel* on the field and probably have the chance to play in the NFL someday, but you will become more successful *outside* of football than you ever are in football."

I wondered if he had some divine knowledge I didn't know about.

This man promised me that no matter how good I was on the football field or how successful my career was in the NFL, he would make sure I developed the skills and characteristics to be even more successful once football ended for me. All athletes worry about this, no matter how many years they play professional sports. What do you do after the glory days of the NFL are over?

After my drug-riddled past, I wanted to play for a coach who could become my friend and mentor. Who cared for me way more than my athletic abilities on the football field. Who was concerned about whether I was happy and whether I would excel after football. And that was exactly how I felt about Coach Hep. I felt at home with him from the first moment we spoke, and I immediately trusted him and believed in him.

I went to Indiana as one of the higher-touted recruits in my class, but this meant there was a great deal of pressure on me to excel, not only from my coaches and teammates, but from the local media and die-hard Hoosier fans all over the country.

In college I started out playing safety, a position I never quite excelled at in high school. I guess they thought I would be good given my combination of size, speed, and strength, but I was anything but good in the beginning.

TACKLE THIS TODAY

Sometimes we have to be pushed out of our comfort zone in order to get better and excel. And it can be painful and difficult. Focus is the key. What have you done lately that's pushed you to the limit? Did you stay focused? Or did you quit? That is the question.

Training camp in August was a nightmare. I had to change my mind-set and recognize that I was now the CEO of my new life. It was up to me—and only me—to take charge of my destiny and turn this training camp into a successful venture. First, I had to adjust to the speed of the game at the collegiate level, as well as the workload. It was night and day in comparison to high school. Plus, I wasn't used to the long meetings and practices. On top of all that, I had new teammates. Finally, I had no friends there yet, and it was the first time I had ever been away from home. Even though I was only four hours away, it was still an adjustment. It was unsettling at first...and lonely. But I was determined to adapt.

As uncomfortable as I was, I resolved to be the best football player I could possibly be. I stayed focused on the task at hand and studied the playbook every chance I got. I interacted with my new coaches and visualized myself making big plays against Ohio State, Michigan, and all the other great teams I would be facing in the Big Ten Conference.

I was determined to not redshirt my freshman year. For all of you who aren't exactly sure what *redshirting* means, it's when an incoming freshman is limited to participating in only practices for the duration of his freshman year, with no live game action. If you end up redshirting, then you get a fifth year to play your sport. For the most part, the decision to redshirt or not comes down to the coaching staff.

If an incoming freshman is going to add tremendous value to a program right away and help his team win, then that player won't redshirt. If someone isn't fully developed yet, whether it's from a mental or physical standpoint, then the coaches will opt to redshirt that player. There is nothing wrong with being redshirted, and in some cases, I have actually seen it play to one's advantage. I didn't want anything to do with redshirting, though, and I let the coaches know that I was eager to contribute immediately.

TACKLE THIS TODAY

The following quote sums up everything I was doing
to improve. What about you?

"An ounce of action is worth a ton

of theory."

—*attributed to Friedrich Engels*

I started to improve and acclimate to the routines and change of pace at the college level, but I still had a long way to go. I began making more plays on the field. The coaching staff decided to move me from safety to outside linebacker. I had to put on some weight, but the change benefited not only me but the whole team. Each day, I focused on getting better with every rep, every practice.

The other team members and I wore shirts with the letters *GBT* engraved on the back. This stood for "Get Better Today." Coach Hep reminded us over and over again, "The only thing that truly matters is to capitalize on the opportunity to live another day and promise ourselves to GBT."

Above all else, if we focused on getting just a little better than the day before, over time, the results would be substantial. I still use the GBT method today and speak about it wherever I go. It doesn't matter if you're in school or what type of work you do. This method can take you to the top and help you become the absolute best at what you do.

Often people seek instant gratification without putting in

the necessary work. They forget the importance of focusing solely on maximizing their life for that particular day—not tomorrow, next week, or next month. Whether you're an executive, a teacher, a salesman, a student, a physician, a nurse, a janitor, a truck driver, a farmer, or a stay-at-home mom or dad, you have the opportunity to improve today.

Every single day you're faced with countless obligations and distractions. It's your job to minimize the distractions and not-so-important things preventing you from becoming your absolute best and being phenomenal in this game of life.

One of the first things you can do is decide that each day, no matter what your circumstances and struggles are, you will find ways to get better. Even if they're baby steps. One little thing each day will add up to big things tomorrow. Some days will consume all your energy. Other days will throw you obstacles. Just know that and be prepared for it. Determine that you will be the leader of your life. The CEO and master of your world.

If you don't make a deliberate effort to get better—to take charge of your life—you won't. Make the decision to GBT. Write it down on a Post-it and place it where you can see it five or six times every day. Pick one area in your life that you want to improve that day and write it down, too. For example:

THINGS YOU CAN TACKLE NOW TO GBT—GET BETTER TODAY

1. **Kindness.** I will do at least one nice thing for someone today without expecting anything in return.

2. **Health.** I will improve my health today by eating more vegetables.

3. **Exercise.** I will get more exercise today by walking for twenty minutes.

4. **Business.** I will do at least one thing to improve my business skills.

5. **Gratitude.** I will be grateful for everything, including the negative, in my life today.

Carry your GBT in your wallet, briefcase, or purse, or program it in your Apple Watch or smartphone. Look at it every chance you get.

Over time, your decision to get better in some area of your life every single day will reap tremendous benefits and drastically increase your success rate. I carried the words "Get Better Today" with me everywhere I went during my whole college career, regardless of whether I was on the field or not. And I still do. It's in my wallet at this moment.

At the end, I had a very average freshman season, but I ended up appearing in eleven total games and totaled twelve tackles on the season.

My best game of the year, and probably the one I'm most proud of, was against Ohio State, which was the number one ranked team in the country at the time. I had eight tackles and one tackle for loss against them while playing with a broken wrist.

I was happy with my freshman season, but I was eager for more and wanted to be great, not just average. So, after freshman year, I devoted my whole summer to training six days a week and worked on getting faster and stronger. I also increased my football IQ by studying Hall of Fame players and watching videos of myself during my freshman year to see where I could improve.

Then one day it happened.

I couldn't believe it.

It wasn't possible.

My world was rocked and turned upside down because of a tragedy. It devastated me.

I still remember the day vividly. It was a warm, humid morning on June 19, 2007. At 6:00 A.M., it was still dark on the football field at Indiana University as we prepared for our off-season morning conditioning.

The coaches called a team meeting, and I immediately knew something was off. *Calling the team together in the middle of a 6:00 A.M. conditioning?* That just didn't happen. When I saw the looks on the coaches' faces, I knew this was no ordinary meeting. Something was wrong.

"I don't know how to say this, team, but...well—" The coach stopped, glanced down at his shoes, and cleared his throat. I could tell he was struggling with his words. "It is with great sadness that I tell you that Coach Hep has passed."

Coach Hoeppner, the man who was like a second father to me, the man who was responsible for me choosing Indiana University, had passed away due to complications from a brain tumor.

No one moved or said a word. You could have heard a pin drop on the floor. Somewhere down the hallway, a door squeaked as it closed. It was as if the world around us was moving in slow motion.

Coach Hep had been out on leave for a while, and we had all heard the rumors about him being sick. But this... this... was *surreal*. It couldn't be true. I couldn't wrap my mind around it. *Coach Hep is dead?* The words sounded wrong. False.

I couldn't breathe. *No, Coach Hep! I came here for you! You believed in me! You took a chance on me!* It felt as though a knife had pierced my chest. I didn't know what to do. I was shocked. At a complete loss for words, I blinked back the tears. I glanced around the room and realized that my teammates felt the exact same way.

Then one of the coaches mentioned a funeral and visitation, but the rest of it was a blur.

Tears streamed down my cheeks. I wiped my nose and got up from my chair, pulling my hoodie over my head in hopes of masking my face. I was worried that my knees would buckle and I would collapse. I plodded out of the meeting room and headed toward the restroom. Once inside, I locked myself in the farthest stall and sobbed.

TACKLE THIS TODAY

When tragedy happens, it's important to hold on to all the good, the love, and the happiness in your life. You will need this to get through the tough times, the tragedies. You will need this to rebuild your strength.

With no exaggeration, this was by far the most difficult moment of my college career. Someone I loved and admired was gone. He had looked me directly in the eyes and told me that I would one day be more successful outside of football than I ever was in football. He was a man who believed in me even when I didn't fully believe in myself. This man was my role model, friend, mentor, leader, coach, father figure, and someone I looked up to in every area of life. Coach Hep took a chance on me. He had believed in me when I needed it most. I loved him for that.

I ached for his wife, Jane, and their children, along with the entire community. I ached for *me*. We had all lost an incredible human being who meant so much to so many people. In fact, I've encountered very few people who have a way with others like Coach Hep did.

After I heard that Coach Hep had died, football didn't really matter to me anymore. A game I loved was now of such little importance in comparison to the game of life. I was depressed. Devastated. It was my first brush with death, and I couldn't make sense of such an incredible person being taken so soon. I talked to my parents and grandparents. They knew how much Coach Hep meant to me, and they tried to give me the emotional support I needed. But when you lose a loved one, it's a very personal experience. No one can take that pain away. You never fully get over it. You learn to accept and cope, but you are forever changed. My teammates were the closest people I had to understanding what I was experiencing.

TACKLE THIS TODAY

Take a moment to go within and feel the pain. It's important to get in touch with your feelings and emotions when a tragedy happens. It's not easy, but it's a vital part of coping and recovering. Are you dealing with a loss or a tragedy? Go within and listen to the gentle messages that are waiting.

The weeks crawled by without Coach Hep. The practice field, the weight room, the stadium felt emptier without him. I hated knowing that I would never get to see him in those places again. Coach Hep and I had become extremely close, and we talked almost every day. Not only did we talk about football, but we also talked about life in general. He took a genuine interest in his players and got to know them as people rather than just last names and numbers. I slowly realized that I could focus on the love and inspiration that I received from Coach Hep, and in that way, I could continue on. I would make him proud of me.

Even in the face of tragedy and adversity, we all have to learn how to go on living. As hard as it was to focus on football, the season was quickly approaching and my teammates and I knew that Coach Hep didn't want "average" on the field. He would want us to give everything we had every single day.

Coach Hep had posted a poem on the wall next to

the GBT sign, along with our team goals, in the meeting room. He recited this poem often, and we came back to it after almost every meeting. Football, just like the game of life, is full of ups and downs. One day you might be on top, and the next day you might get knocked flat on your face. The following poem has forever changed my perspective on failure and what adversity, persistence, and success really mean.

Keep Going

When things go wrong, as they sometimes will,
And the road you're trudging seems all up hill,
When the funds are low and the debts are high
And you want to smile, but you have to sigh,
When care is pressing down a bit,
Rest, if you must—but don't you quit.

Life is queer with its twists and turns,
As every one of us sometimes learns,
And many a failure turns about
When he might have won had he stuck it out.
Don't give up, though the pace seems slow,
You may succeed with another blow.

Often the goal is nearer than
It seems to a faint and faltering man.
Often the struggler has given up
When he might have captured the victor's cup,

And he learned too late, when the night slipped down,
How close he was to the golden crown.

Success is failure turned inside out—
The silver tint of the clouds of doubt,
And you never can tell how close you are,
It may be near when it seems afar;
Stick to the fight when you're hardest hit—
It's when things seem worse that you mustn't quit.
                                        —Edgar A. Guest

I recited that poem every day for the rest of my college career in memory of Coach Hep. And even now, when times are rough and I think I'm failing or some tragedy has hit, I read that poem. The tears always well up in my eyes when I remember Coach Hep.

During the 2007 season, the year he passed away, Coach Hep was certainly with us on the field every game we played. For the first time since 1993, the Indiana Hoosiers played in a bowl game and achieved Coach Hep's dream of "playing thirteen," which meant playing in twelve regular-season games plus a bowl game.

I still get emotional when I think of that year. The emotion, passion, and pain that we experienced as a team accompanied us as we ran out on the football field to play every Saturday. We all recognized that Coach Hep was the reason our team was so dynamic and special. We remembered that Coach Hep told us that the best teams and organizations work collectively toward achieving something bigger than individual awards. And that was exactly what we did that year. We carried Coach Hep's heart with us in every game.

I ended my sophomore season with 42 total tackles as a backup middle linebacker. It put me in position to be the starting middle linebacker junior year. I had a great junior season. I started all 12 games and led the team with 89 tackles and tied a school record for most sacks in a game, when I recorded 4 sacks against Central Michigan.

That great season was followed up by an even better one my senior year. I was selected as game captain five times. I started all 12 games as middle linebacker and led the team again in tackles with 108. I ended my career with 251 tackles, 139 solo, 10.5 sacks (73 yards), 22.5 tackles for loss (99 yards), 3 interceptions, and 3 fumble recoveries.

Sure, the football stats were wonderful, but after my 2009 senior season, I received the award I'm still the most proud of—the Howard Brown Award. It's given to the player who exemplifies leadership, courage, and a strong work ethic. *Me. The kid who was once too weak to face himself. The kid who used to do anything to be accepted. The kid whose only work ethic involved stealing to get high.*

I know Coach Hep looked down on me and smiled when I won the Howard Brown Award. And I know he was proud of me. I accepted the award in his honor.

As I finish this chapter, I'll leave you with this: "GBT, my friends." I'm sure Coach Hep is busy having the time of his life traveling in the *Far Country* right now, but I'm sure he'd smile and chime in with me and say, "GBT, my friends."

Thank you, Coach Hep, for everything.

YOUR OWN PERSONAL GAME PLAN
TO PUT INTO ACTION

1. Follow your instinct and heart. When I chose to play football at Indiana University, many people couldn't understand my decision. The thing is, it wasn't for *them* to understand. It was in my heart. It was in my gut. Indiana was the school for me. I'm glad I listened to my inner voice, my gut instinct. It was one of the best decisions of my life. More often than not, you know what's best for you deep down in your heart. Give yourself permission to trust your gut instinct and follow your heart.

2. Create a GBT agreement. Adopt Coach Hep's motto—"Get Better Today"—and put this into practice every day. I discuss it a lot in this book because it's so important. If you adopt this mind-set, you'll be challenged when you experience failures and hardships. It will be rough, and there will be days you won't want to get out of bed. But you can do it. What has helped me is a binding GBT agreement that I wrote down for myself. It creates a sense of urgency in my life and takes my motivation to a new level. Here's a real example of a binding agreement:

(Today's date)

I, Matt Mayberry, abide by the terms of this contract. I vouch to give my very best toward everything I put my hands on. I will uplift and encourage everyone I encounter. My time will be spent wisely while directing all my focus and energy on my most important tasks. Everything that is placed on my "things to do" for today will be done passionately and quickly. I will learn something

new and grow somehow, someway. Just for today, I will
be great and get better.

I keep this contract with me everywhere I go. I have one copy in my briefcase, one on my phone, and one in my wallet. When I'm feeling sluggish or unmotivated to go the extra mile, I glance at this agreement with myself, and my mental attitude changes immediately. Feel free to create something similar or explore different methods of your own. There is no right or wrong way of doing this. The only thing that matters is that you create something that will encourage you to GBT each and every day.

3. Cherish your loved ones. Life is extremely short, so love and cherish those you love most each and every moment you can. Coach Hep's death was the first time I lost someone I was close to. It crushed me, but it taught me the importance of appreciating and loving people while they're still here and not waiting for a tragedy to realize how precious life is. Tell those you love how much they mean to you and how much you appreciate them. And do it often. I so desperately wish I could have just one more conversation with Coach Hep so I could tell him how much I love him and how grateful I am to have been his friend and a Hoosier while he was coach. Somehow, though, I think he knows.

Chapter Five

D-DAY: THE PHONE CALL THAT CHANGED MY LIFE

It is not the critic who counts; not the man who points out how the strong man stumbles or where the doer of deeds could have done them better.

The credit belongs to the man who is actually in the arena, whose face is marred by dust and sweat and blood; who strives valiantly; who errs, who comes short again and again, because there is no effort without error and shortcoming; but who does actually strive to do the deeds; who knows great enthusiasms, the great devotions; who spends himself in a worthy cause; who at the best knows in the end the triumph of high achievement, and who at the worst, if he fails, at least fails while daring greatly, so that his place shall never be with those cold and timid souls who neither know victory nor defeat.

—*Theodore Roosevelt*

This day was finally here! It was beyond anything I ever dreamed. It was D-day. Draft Day.

After my years as an award-winning Hoosier athlete at

Indiana University, I was now ready for the big leagues. The NFL. This would be one of the most important days in my life. I was about to be drafted to the NFL. I was sure of it. I had been sweating it out at home for days. That morning I had to keep my mind focused. I had to know that I would succeed. Everything in the world seemed to be at stake—and life, as I knew it, was about to change forever. Or so I hoped.

The only thing I could think about was when I was a little child driving my mother absolutely crazy while wearing my Walter Payton jersey and pretending I was playing for the 1985 Super Bowl Champion Chicago Bears. I'm from the Chicago area, so I grew up loving Walter Payton and that drew me to the Bears, but I loved other teams, as well. My dream was simply to play professional sports. And now, I was actually about to live that dream with the NFL. All the hard work and sacrifices that my parents and I had made to get to this point were finally starting to pay off.

For me, D-day was an excruciating experience I'll never forget. Leading up to the draft, I was projected to go somewhere between the fourth and seventh rounds. There are countless draft experts, and it seemed they all had something different to say about my talent, ability, and projection on where I would get drafted.

Not long before D-day, I had participated in Ignition Athletic Performance Group's Pro Player Training program at a facility in Cincinnati. As they post on their website, "Ignition is a worldwide leader in sports performance training with clients from twenty-three countries." They train athletes from all major professional sports with a focus on speed, agility, and strength, and they are widely known for training athletes who go into the draft.

I was with the best of the best, and I trained with several standout NFL players. The training was intense; all we did was eat, train, and sleep. We lived and breathed the game. You had to if you wanted to reach the next level.

The staff at Ignition does an excellent job of preparing you mentally and physically for the next level. They've worked with a lot of NFL linebackers, and I was grateful for the experience. I was focused on the physical through and through. I worked out by myself even after the others had left the gym for the day. I shadowboxed in the steam room. I stared into the mirror and flexed my muscles. Like a Roman gladiator, pumped and ready to charge others in the arena, I was ready for the NFL.

At the end of the training program, Ted, one of the trainers, a kind but strict and disciplined man, pulled me aside and said, "You know what? I've seen a lot of linebackers come here to train for the draft, but because of your outstanding strength and talents, you might just be the best of all of them."

I shook his hand and smiled big. This was what I wanted to hear. It gave me the extra boost and assurance I needed. Yeah, I was going to be picked. I could hardly wait!

To add to my confidence, in the days leading up to the draft, a frenzy was building in the sports world, and I was already big news. Sports announcers and NFL analysts in the media, including ESPN and other sports shows, discussed my exceptional opportunities. It seemed like all the sports analysts were rooting for me and supporting me in my efforts.

However, friends and past teammates offered warnings.

"Matt, you can't really expect anything. You just never know how this is going to go." I barely listened to what they said. They were downers—negative. Instead, I focused on the good news and accolades I heard from the analysts on the media outlets.

One sample of what I heard sports analysts and reporters say was: "Matt Mayberry is a week away from one of the biggest events of his life to date: the 2010 NFL Draft. Mayberry, who grew up in Chicago, a team captain and middle linebacker from Indiana University, was a recipient of the 2009 Howard Brown Award. He's now preparing for life as a professional NFL football player."

Another sample was: "Mayberry's season at Indiana University was exceptional. He led the team in tackles—and finished Top Five in the Big Ten with tackles, completing three interceptions and five sacks. He's surely a linebacker to watch during this season's draft."

I heard these kinds of accolades over and over. My head swelled with ego. I knew there was no way I'd fail. I would be picked.

Tim Cary, featured columnist for *Bleacher Report*, called to interview me the week before the draft. "What are your plans for watching the draft this coming weekend?"

"Nothing too special," I said. "I'll be in Chicago relaxing. Just spending the day with my family."

"How many different teams have you talked to, or worked out for, during the predraft process?" asked Cary.

"I've spoken to just about every team, except a few," I explained, "and I've worked out and visited more than a handful. The Bears and Patriots are already out there in the media, but the other teams I've visited with have asked to keep it quiet, so I've got to stick to their requests on that one."

I went on to explain that my predraft workout preparation at Ignition was intense, beginning at 8:00 A.M. and ending at 7:00 P.M. My training involved speed work, followed by position work and then hitting the weights in the afternoon, with rehab-type stuff to prevent injuries, and recovery methods.

TACKLE THIS TODAY

When you tackle anything in life, whether it's sports, education, or business, it will help if you put yourself on a training and/or an improvement program. Are you training in any area of your life right now? What could you improve?

Even then, while interviewing with sportscasters and newspaper journalists, I emphasized that I thrived on speed and believed that my work ethic and relentless positive attitude were second to none. I took pride in working as hard as possible every single day.

Simply put, I knew I would be drafted.

D-day finally came in April 2010 on a gray, rainy Saturday afternoon amid newly budding trees in Chicago. I was at my parents' home, waiting, since I wasn't a guaranteed first-round draft pick. Those players received a huge sign-on bonus and anxiously waited in the greenroom at Radio City Music Hall in New York City for their names to be called. With friends already in the NFL and former teammates preparing me months in advance for what to expect today, I decided not to have a party. Instead, it was quiet in our house. My grandparents and a select few friends stopped by at random times to see how things were going. My grandparents brought my favorite chocolate chip cookies and offered me "good vibes and good energy." My aunt and her daughters knocked on the door with a poster that said, "Matt Mayberry is #1."

In many ways, it was like an ordinary Saturday, except for the energy, the tension in the air, and the expectancy we were all trying to ignore.

I was nervous and could barely sit still. I didn't want to stay glued to the TV, though, and the only time I watched the NFL Draft was when my teammate Rodger Saffold, an offensive tackle from Indiana University, was drafted in the second round, thirty-third overall, to the St. Louis Rams.

I cheered loudly, "Yeah, Big Rodg! Hoo-Hoo-Hoosiers!"

The second one was Jammie Kirlew, another Indiana University alumni, drafted by the Denver Broncos. I was very excited for him and was positive that somewhere in the seventh round, I would get selected, too. I knew many of the teams were looking for linebackers. So there was no way I wouldn't be picked.

After seeing these former Indiana University teammates get selected, I smiled for the first time that day. I was extremely proud and excited for these two young men, as I knew firsthand exactly what they had sacrificed and how hard they had worked.

Most people looking from the outside in seem to think

that athletes wake up one day and have this incredible amount of talent and ability. In some cases, that's absolutely the truth. But the fact of the matter is that only a very small percentage of athletes have the God-given talent of a LeBron James or a Peyton Manning. Even those two athletes work their butts off and have a work ethic that is second to none. But the majority of professional athletes have to work extra hard to develop their special talents. They are the ones who have a gut-wrenching desire to be the best and reach their fullest potential no matter how hard they have to work.

On D-day, we were all trying to play it cool, but everyone in my family—my grandparents, Mom, Dad, and my brother, Gary—was nervous and anxious. We roamed from room to room, trying to calm our nerves as we waited for someone to pick me in the draft.

Grampa Dee tried to encourage me. "Just hang in there, son. You'll be picked. You've worked hard for this. You'll do great. I know you will."

I nodded. I knew that Grampa Dee understood all too well the pain and suffering I had experienced to get to this moment. And I knew all too well how much he believed in me.

No one in my family was glued to the television waiting for my name to be called. We were all trying to stay busy.

My grandparents finally left and told us to call them as soon as we heard anything. Friends who randomly stopped by to say hello and good luck left with all their good wishes. Dad and Gary went to go work out in the gym.

Dad wanted this for me. He believed this would be a major

positive turning point in my life, and if I wasn't picked—*well, things might not go so well*…based on my past mistakes and decisions when I got angry or upset about something. I had not always handled my temper very well in those situations. Dad has one of the strongest work ethics I know. As an ironworker, he's the kind of man that built America. He works six days a week including Saturdays, but on D-day, he got off work at 1:00 P.M., because he knew what this day meant to me and he wanted to be there.

I put on my running shoes, threw a sweatshirt over my head, and jogged out the door. I ran hard for two miles, then walked another mile. I started to question myself. *Am I good enough to play in the NFL?*

I reflected on life, football, all the hard work, my sacrifices, and my parents' sacrifices. *What's my purpose in life?* I questioned a lot of things. I was only twenty-two, and I suddenly felt like I had nothing to give—like an old washed-up has-been.

Am I going to get picked, or what? Have I failed?

I know now that we should never anticipate the worst and add strong feelings to those anticipations. Adding emotion to imagination is a powerful creative process that we should use *only* for envisioning the outcome we really want. We should feel it, see it, smell it, taste it. When you put feelings into your imagination, anything is possible.

So, don't imagine something negative. I knew that. And yet with the tension of the moment, I did exactly that. Don't do what I did. Anything is better than adding vision and emotion to the worst-case scenario. But at the time, I slipped into that dark place. I tried to shake it, to run it off as my feet pounded block after block.

TACKLE THIS TODAY

When you imagine the worst, you can almost ensure the worst will happen. We create our world with our thoughts and imagination. What are you imagining today? Be careful that you don't slip into a dark place that's hard to climb out of.

After my run, I returned to the house and took a quick shower. Then I sat down in the living room and watched the draft. In that moment, I was focused as if my life depended on it.

There are seven rounds in the NFL Draft, and once my teammate Jammie Kirlew was selected in the seventh round and my name wasn't called yet, I began getting upset. Disbelief filled me. Would I be passed over? What was happening here?

All the linebackers were getting taken off the board. They were being drafted. And my name still wasn't called.

I was definitely starting to get more anxious because, deep down, I believed I would be off the board somewhere in the fourth or fifth round, especially given the conversations I'd had with some of the teams I had privately worked out for before the draft.

There was no way to know exactly what was going to happen throughout this whole process. The NFL is unpredictable, and the draft is no exception. I just had to wait it out. The suspense was killing me.

I tried to stay positive, but I couldn't help wondering what would happen if my name didn't get called during the entire draft. Suddenly that possibility was becoming real, and I knew I'd be devastated. I would be such a huge disappointment to my family and coaches. A disappointment to myself. A big, fat failure.

The draft can be a long and dreadful process, and that was exactly what it had become for me. Pick after pick, I still hadn't heard my name called. When the end of the seventh round finally came, I was past anxious. I was angry. Upset. Frustrated. Because I knew I wasn't seventh-round talent. Something had clearly happened. For some reason, I had been passed over. What would happen now?

I had no idea. I had certainly not prepared for this possibility. Not after all the hard work, not after being a media darling. As the minutes passed, I compared myself to other players, with how fast I ran at my pro day at Indiana University. I was one of the leading tacklers in the Big Ten Conference, and I had completed three interceptions my senior year as a linebacker. No one could possibly tell me that I should still be on the board this long.

My other thoughts were once again more negative and self-diminishing. With four picks left to go in the seventh round and as each pick ended, I questioned my ability and whether or not I could play in the National Football League at all. I doubted myself the way I had during my darkest days.

Do I really have what it takes to achieve at this level of performance? My record was great, but Draft Day was proving to be my undoing. Now, I suddenly doubted my ability and achievements more than ever before.

Athletes are normally very confident men and women, especially those reaching the pinnacle of their sports. However, for me, in this particular moment, I was drained emotionally, mentally, and spiritually, and I had very little confidence left.

I remembered those who had told me I would never make something of myself because I had once been a drug addict, a wayward youth. Yeah, there was that. I was haunted by past failures.

What hurt the most was seeing other linebackers selected before me. I knew them, and I felt they couldn't bring the value and skill to a team that I could. Apparently, all the teams believed the exact opposite, because players with lesser achievements were selected while I was still sitting on the couch in my parents' living room.

With only three picks left in the last round of the 2010 NFL Draft, I turned off the TV. Dad and Gary didn't say a word. Mom was busy in the kitchen cooking dinner, but she knew. Everyone knew to leave me alone.

Without speaking to anyone, I headed upstairs and threw myself down on my bed. I turned over on my left side and propped my head up with my left hand. I reached over to my nightstand and grabbed some of the fan mail that I had received from die-hard Hoosier football fans all over the country. Throughout this whole process, I had remained as calm as possible. But now, I was crumbling. Were all my hard work, struggles, and dreams truly coming to this dreadful end?

Looking through the fan letters was an emotional time for me. They spoke to me. Just holding them in my hands helped me remember who I was. I began to read. Letter after letter encouraged me, and I was shocked to find tears rolling freely down both cheeks.

Matt, because of you, my son is now off of drugs and get-
ting into football. He's hoping to get a scholarship to play
football in college like you did, and he would have never
had the motivation to do so without your story. Thank
you from the bottom of my heart.

Love, the mother of a drug addict

During the draft process, I had stayed as strong as possible, but because I hadn't been selected, I allowed negative emotions to annihilate my soul and diminish my self-belief. Instead of letting the circumstances motivate me to do something about it, I was letting them derail me from my goals. I felt devastated and about as low as I had ever felt—and I knew only I could change this situation. But I didn't know what to do. Hope was draining quickly from the depths of my being.

I read a few more fan letters. The encouraging words seeped between the cracks of my shattered spirit like glue. I began to not only feel but believe in their impact. I focused on the inner strength that had been in me all along. I sat up on my bed, took the tail of my T-shirt, and wiped my face dry. Reading how I had impacted people's lives in an encouraging, positive way gave me the morale boost I needed.

I allowed myself to release the anger and regained a sense of determination. Once again, as I had learned to do many times before, I took control. Anger can be a creative tool if used in a positive way. It's a higher emotion energetically than the despair and sadness and self-pity I had been wallowing in. I had to overcome the hurt and disappointment that none of the teams had picked me. I had to use the anger as fuel, release it, and let it motivate me to action. I had to get ready to work and prove to every single team that passed on me that they were wrong. And slowly, the passion reignited like fire within me. I remembered who I was. I remembered my goals. My dreams. My determination. What I could do!

THINGS YOU CAN TACKLE NOW TO HELP YOU REMEMBER WHO YOU ARE

1. **Reaffirm your goals.** When your goals and dreams fall apart, you may forget who you are. How strong you are. How committed you are. Take out your index cards where your dreams and goals are listed. Take out the GBT card that has Coach Hep's motto: "Get Better Today." Remember, you are a dreamer, a goal builder, and, most important, a goal achiever. You are someone who can tackle life at its most difficult and come out a winner, a survivor.

2. **Focus on your achievements.** Make a list of all the things you have achieved. For me, it was the 2009 Howard Brown Award at Indiana University and the Division I college scholarship. And it was all the letters I had received from fans and people who knew about my high school drug addiction. I made a list of the things I had worked hard for and the triumphs and successes. I remembered all the good things that were happening instead of dwelling on the negative.

3. **Remember your loved ones.** Make a list of all the people who love you and all the people you love. I thought about my parents, my grandparents, my brother, Gary, and especially Grampa Dee. I thought about Coach Hep and my buddies in football, and the happy memories we shared helped

me to remember that I was *more* than this rejection by the NFL. I could not let myself be defined by this.

4. Use anger as a positive, motivating energy. Tell yourself and the world that you will take charge of that anger and be the master of your life. The leader and CEO of your life. And that you will not let anyone or anything make you feel inadequate. You deserve the best life. You deserve to be happy and successful. We simply do not have to live in the shadows of what could have been if we focus on *what can be* and we allow it to manifest through hard work and determination.

5. Take action. Make up your mind to do something to turn the negative into a positive—some small action that will move you closer to your dreams. First, I ran and worked off some of the negative energy. Then I read some fan letters to give me encouragement and faith in myself. Next, after I began to believe in myself again, I remembered that I could be signed as a free agent. I had to believe that someone would want me. You can do this, too. Figure out a way to regroup and attack your plan from a different angle. Just don't forget who you are.

I sprang up from my bed as fast as lightning, determined that I would take charge of this situation. Yes, I wanted to be drafted, but if not, I could still sign as a free agent—*if anyone wanted me. Surely someone would want me!* I couldn't change what had just occurred, but I could take positive action for the future now! I could stay focused. I could control what I was going to do. It was an important lesson that I have applied time and again whenever I have failed at something important. Sometimes things happen that are simply beyond your control, so you must take control of what you can.

I called my agent, Michael Boyer, to help me analyze my next step. "What's going on?" I asked, my heart pounding hard and loud like a thousand drums.

"It's not over. We have some options." His voice was firm and confident. "You can sign as a free agent once the draft ends, and sometimes that's actually better, assuming you have a few teams that want you. Then you get to choose. If you're drafted, you have no choice."

"Does anyone want me?" I asked in a voice so low it was almost a whisper.

"There are four teams who are interested in signing you that I think would be perfect for you."

"What do you mean?" I was barely able to breathe.

"In fact, I've received more than ten calls from NFL teams expressing their interest in signing you as an undrafted free agent." I could hear the smile in his voice. And just like that, everything was in motion again.

"What?" *Really? Really?* My heart lifted big-time.

"Yep, and the four teams that I think are the best suited for you are the Chicago Bears, Atlanta Falcons, Houston Texans, and Tennessee Titans."

"Connect me with the Chicago Bears." I didn't have to think twice about it.

Two minutes later, I was on the phone with Bob Babich, the linebackers coach for the Chicago Bears. I knew Bob from my visit and private workout with the Bears leading up to the draft. He was a guy who loved athletic linebackers. Truth be told, that's really what the Chicago Bears' long history of great linebackers consists of—athletes who can run fast and hard and are agile enough to be outstanding in pass coverage.

"I know you're upset that you didn't get picked up in the draft," Bob Babich said, "but be reassured that it doesn't matter where you start. It's all about where you finish."

"Yeah, it's true. I'm disappointed about the draft," I told him.

"Being picked in the draft isn't everything. You have options. And, Matt, Chicago is the place you should be. It's your hometown. Your family and friends are in Chicago. And Brian Urlacher and Lance Briggs—you can learn from them."

He was selling me, but I didn't need his sales pitch.

We were on the phone for a total of three minutes, and the whole time Bob explained to me why I should choose the Bears over the other teams that wanted to sign me. It was music to my ears.

"Look, Matt, you'll receive the same opportunities to make the playing roster as someone who was drafted."

"Bob, everything sounds good. Tell you what; I'll give you a call after I talk to my agent. Can I call you back in the next ten minutes?"

"Sure, fine."

This was an important decision for me, and this call was extremely reassuring, but I wanted to think about it for a few moments. When we hung up, I suddenly thought about all the legendary players who went undrafted and then created Hall of Fame careers.

Next, I received a call from the linebackers coach for the Houston Texans. He was pumped up and excited. I could hear his enthusiasm through the phone. "You'll fit right in here with the Houston Texans. We really need someone like you with your size and speed ratio. You'd also have the opportunity to participate on special teams."

I recognized that the more versatile you were, the more you could do for a team and the greater your chances were to actually make that team.

"Thanks for your interest," I said, "but I already know where I'm going to sign."

I knew deep down that my decision was a good one. My vision was coming into clear focus. There was light and hope and the promise of great days ahead. This was what I was breathing in and focusing on.

I hung up the phone, and the Atlanta Falcons called me. I promptly told them the same things I had told the Texans. "Thank you, but no."

Then I called my agent. "I've made up my mind. I want to sign with the Bears."

"Congratulations! It's a great decision. I believe in you and can't wait for you to prove to yourself and everyone else how great you are when training camp comes around. I'm happy for you."

"Thanks, Michael, for your belief in me," I said. Tears filled my eyes. The day had been an emotional roller coaster of the biggest sort, and this was an overwhelming moment. "I won't let you down."

I called Bob Babich and the Chicago Bears and told them, "I want to become a Chicago Bear."

"That is fantastic news," Bob said. "I'm happy to hear this and can't wait to work with you."

Bob's enthusiasm was contagious. Sure, I had most definitely wanted this phone call to take place during the draft; it would have been ideal. But that was not the way it happened. First I had to take charge inwardly, as we all do. Nonetheless, this was the phone call that would change my entire life.

I grabbed the Chicago Bears baseball cap that was hanging on my bedpost and put it on. I went downstairs and tried to act as nonchalant as ever—as though nothing had happened.

I walked into the den where Gary and my father sat on the sofa, huddled around the TV.

Gary looked up with eyes big and wide. "What?"

Then Dad stared at me with a question written all over his face, his eyes pleading to know what was happening.

"I went with the Bears," I said as calmly as I could.

My brother shot up from the sofa and gave me a high five.

Dad shook his head. "I knew you'd get a team…I mean, I had hoped…and, well…the *Chicago Bears*! I'm proud of you, son." I wasn't sure, but I could have sworn he had tears in his eyes.

I went to the kitchen. Mom stood there at the stove and turned around slowly.

"Mom, I'm a Chicago Bear." I tipped my hat to her.

She dropped the dish towel and threw her arms around me, crying, "Oh, my gosh! I'm so happy for you!"

I laughed and hugged her. "I still have a lot of work to do."

"I know, but this is just wonderful," she said.

Feeling as though the weight of the world had just been lifted off my shoulders, I tweeted the news and posted a status on my Facebook page announcing that I was officially a Chicago Bear. I thought, *I'm a Chicago Bear! I'm a Chicago Bear! I'm not a drug addict any longer. I'm not a failure after all!*

I received calls from media outlets, and congratulatory text messages and calls from high school friends, college teammates, supervisors, mentors, family members, and fans poured in. The incredible support was almost overwhelming. I enjoyed the messages for a good hour, but in the back of my mind, I knew that I hadn't done anything yet—I had not actually proven a darn thing to anyone. I still had a long road ahead of me.

As an undrafted free agent, you have to prove yourself that much more to the coaching staff and front office executives. From all the stories I had heard from friends and former teammates who were already in the NFL, I knew that nothing in this business was ever guaranteed. There were a lot of challenges ahead of me, but I felt well seasoned in tackling adversity, and I was ready.

That night, after all the celebrating had died down, my brother, my parents, and I sat around the kitchen table eating my mom's famous ravioli, discussing my good fortune of truly being a Chicago Bear. Euphoria enveloped me. I was filled with gratitude. Love. Happiness. All the struggle, training, discipline, and hard work were finally paying off. All my parents' efforts to help me and get me to this point were worth it.

Outside, the balmy wind warbled across the yard. The breeze carried its own melody and brought with it the neighborhood sounds of traffic and barking dogs into our home. Life was good.

Coming up next was the actual signing of my new NFL contract with the Chicago Bears, which would include a sign-on bonus, followed by my rookie training camp. I didn't think anything could ever upset this euphoria I was feeling.

Yet life would continue to do what it does—challenging the high of this day with surprises and failures waiting around every corner.

YOUR OWN PERSONAL GAME PLAN
TO PUT INTO ACTION

1. **Ask better questions**. If you want a better life, ask yourself better questions about your future. If you want to turn failures into extraordinary gifts, then asking the right questions will help you change your life. It can also help save failing marriages and relationships. It can be a tool to build stronger financial support for your family. It can aid in your evolution. When you're faced with failure or some adversity, the quality of your questions matters even more. Most people think negatively about a problem or failure. They beat themselves up over something they did wrong. And they ask the wrong questions. For example, when the draft was nearing the end and my name still was uncalled, I started believing the worst. *Am I a good athlete? Am I even good enough to play in the NFL?* That's a prime example of the types of negative questions we ask ourselves when we fail. It wasn't until I tuned out the negative noise and asked myself different questions that my perspective changed. *C'mon, is this truly the end of the world?* Of course not. I tried to cheer myself up: *Hey, I didn't get drafted. It happens. It's a business.* That didn't make me feel any better, but it did improve my attitude. This new perspective fueled the fire in me and gave me a burning desire to prove my worth to every team, general manager, and owner who passed on me in the draft. My perspective changed because of the questions I started to ask myself.

2. **What's your unhappiness question?** Think of the last time you were unhappy about an event that didn't go the way you wanted or a time you felt like a complete failure. Did you ask yourself: *Do I even have the ability to do this? What did I get myself into? Why did*

I even try in the first place when I knew this was going to happen? These types of questions are self-diminishing and negative. They will leave you in a mediocre place where negativity dwells. The kinds of questions we ask ourselves determine the final outcome.

3. Failure is not a final event. When someone experiences a failure, they view it as something final. As if you can't change your world. But when they question themselves about that failure, there is a lack of quality in their questions. If you get lazy and ask yourself the same lousy, nonquality questions, you'll continue to get the same lousy results. There is no way around it.

4. Be intentional. One of the best ways I have found to end the negative and self-diminishing questions is by being *intentional* about it. Ask questions that will empower you and help you find solutions to your problems. When I returned to my parents' house after my run and read through the fan mail I had received over the years, something magical happened. The emotional letters prompted me to think long and hard about some of my past successes. In turn, I asked quality questions such as: *Is this the end of the world?* Of course not. Knowing that I had many options empowered me and made me feel good about my successes. The negative thoughts began to disappear, and I started to believe in myself again.

5. Believe in yourself. You must believe in yourself and your abilities to create a life of high achievement. Can you point out an extremely successful person who doesn't greatly believe in themselves? It's not going to happen. Steve Jobs, Martin Luther King Jr., Michael Jordan, Elon Musk, and Mark Cuban are just a few highly successful individuals who have benefited from the power of self-belief. It's because of their willingness to get up again and again when they fail or experience a setback while pursuing their dreams.

You may not have fan mail to read as you reminisce about your past successes. However, you certainly can implement the following steps, which will encourage you when you're feeling disappointed.

- **Create a picture book.** Find old pictures, newspaper headlines, quotes from your mentors and heroes, Facebook albums, Twitter messages, trophies, and anything else to remind yourself of a past success or an incredibly happy moment in your life. Put them in a laminated binder. What you include in your picture book is entirely up to you. The whole essence of creating a picture book is to activate, inspire, and ignite your mind, body, and spirit. When you're feeling down, the pictures will take you back to those special moments in an instant.

- **Embrace the power of belief and talk to yourself like you're a champion.** My friend and best-selling author Jon Gordon always says, "Talk to yourself more than you listen to yourself." You may think this sounds silly, but for just one day or one week, try talking to yourself like you're a champion instead of complaining that you're a victim. I guarantee you'll be amazed by the results. It reinforces the power of belief. If you keep telling yourself you're a champion, you'll begin to believe it, and once you believe it, your life starts changing.

- **Affirmations.** With power and conviction, repeat affirmations. They could be: "I am the greatest at what I do," or "There is nothing I can't do when I fully commit myself." They might include: "There is nothing ordinary about me. I am a champion." If you don't believe in yourself, there is no way you can expect anyone else to believe in you.

Chapter Six

THE NITTY-GRITTY: I'M A CHICAGO BEAR! TRAINING TO BE AN NFL PLAYER

I know of no more encouraging fact than the unquestionable ability of man to elevate his life by conscious endeavor.

—Henry David Thoreau

The moment was here. I was fully aware of every sound, smell, and movement. Every sense was on high alert. The blood pumped through my veins. This was one of my major goals realized. In action. I had arrived.

I walked into the locker room to change into my workout clothes for the first time. Jockstraps, T-shirts, socks, and towels were slung on the door handles of the lockers. The smells of sweat, soap, dirt, and pure excitement filled my nostrils. *I'm a rookie for the Chicago Bears!* Part of me could hardly believe it, but the other part acted like it was business as usual and no big deal. As an undrafted free agent rookie, I didn't want to show too much sentiment, even though my emotions were bubbling under the surface. Outwardly, I was there for one reason only: to work hard and prove my worth.

The team, especially the rookies, could hardly wait to get out on the field for our first practice for the upcoming season. I was still extremely pissed, as well as confused, as to how I had been *undrafted*, but I had turned that anger into a commitment to becoming the best football player I could possibly be. I've learned that anger can be a constructive tool if used properly. Like all emotions, it has its purposes. When one takes anger and uses that energy for achievement, it makes all the difference. The best revenge, the best remedy for anger, is success. So that was what I decided to do. I planned to work harder than I had ever worked before to make the Chicago Bears roster.

It was finally time to suit up as a Chicago Bear. It was what I had been waiting for all my life. This would be my first challenge as a professional football player at the rookie minicamp. And it was an important one.

After the NFL Draft, there are a few weeks of downtime before all the rookies report to their team's headquarters for a special minicamp weekend. Ours was held at Halas Hall in Lake Forest, Illinois, at the Chicago Bears' headquarters. At the camp, the rookies compete, run drills, and perform as professionals in front of the coaches for the very first time.

One of the most memorable moments was when I received my Chicago Bears practice gear. With the football jersey on my lap, I sat on the bench and held the helmet with the famous *C*, slowly turning it around and around. I marveled at the wonder of it. *I'm a Chicago Bear!* While growing up, I had seen the football gear on the players, and now it dawned on me how special this moment was. I thought about my parents, my dark past that still haunted me, and the truly amazing people who had assisted me along the way. I was motivated to make them proud and happy. From here on out, I would represent my city, family, and friends to the fullest.

I replayed my happy childhood memories watching the great running back Walter Payton, nicknamed Sweetness, who played for the Bears for thirteen seasons. When I was a little boy, he was my idol. I'd pretend I was Walter Payton and run around the yard, throwing a football with Grampa Dee or Dad. Would I be as good as Walter Payton? Would I play for thirteen seasons? After a few moments, I got up from the bench and finished getting dressed.

I was ready. I headed out to the practice field, taking in everything around me. I wanted to relish all of it—the sunlight streaming over the grass on the field, the coaches and other rookies already at work. I was aware of a slight wind that drifted on the air.

TACKLE THIS TODAY

Slow down and enjoy the small moments, especially the ones that include victory and accomplishments. Hang on to those memories when times become difficult, because they will help you rebound and recover with strength.

Even though I would work as hard as I could to make the team and prove my worth, the NFL would not last forever. I'd been warned by former and even current players about how short their careers were. But no matter what happened, I would savor the moment.

I don't have many regrets, but in college, I unfortunately missed out on some very special moments because I was focused on the "next level of football" and playing in the NFL. Many people are so ambitious that they completely forget how to enjoy living in the moment, and I was extremely determined to not let that happen now. That was easier said than done, though.

Many times throughout my life, I have focused on "the next big thing." It's a major blessing and a curse that I'm so ambitious. It's a blessing because I'm willing to do whatever it takes to achieve a goal or a dream. I have never limited my thinking due to a lack of knowledge or resources.

On the flip side, it's also a curse, because while I'm always focused on achieving a major goal, I end up spending very little time in the present and appreciating the entire experience. I have to constantly remind myself to stop and enjoy the journey.

I'm sure you understand what I mean. Most people seem to concentrate on future happiness. And then there are the ones I call the "Remember whens?" who long for their past glory days. I've seen this in sports as well as in business. The majority of us live in a liminal state—not quite brave enough to be alive in the present moment but aware that it's there. Sometimes we catch a glimpse of it. The smell of a locker room before you go out onto the ball field, the sunset that's streaked in reds and oranges, a child's laughter in a crowded airport, or the dazzling joy of our partner's smile. Perhaps people believe if they live in the present, they'll forget their past. Or maybe people worry that if they neglect the future, they'll end up failing.

Self-help guru Junia Bretas said this about living in the moment: "If you are depressed, you are living in the past. If you are anxious, you are living in the future. If you are living at peace, you are living in the present."*

Don't get stuck in your past, and don't get stuck in your future. Focus on where you are right now and all that you need to do to achieve the future you want.

TACKLE THIS TODAY

Being present means that your focus is true and constant. But memories can also serve to help you stay on course and remind you of all that you have learned on your journey. What memories do you cherish that have helped you on your journey? What memories will you take with you to help build your dreams?

I find it fascinating that there are certain things about people and life that do not change over thousands of years.

*http://philosiblog.com/2013/06/19/if-you-are-depressed-you-are-living-in -the-past-if-you-are-anxious-living-in-the-future-if-you-are-at-peace-you-are -living-in-the-moment/

And I'm learning that truly being present does not mean that we forsake our memories and our past or that we forget about planning for our future. If you think about it, the present moment is all that we truly own. Our future is unknown and precarious. We are not guaranteed any tomorrows. Losing Coach Hep while I was in college was a huge reminder of this. In fact, anytime I lose a loved one, I am reminded of it.

Regardless of how big your dream or end goal may be, don't fall into the trap of neglecting the present moment. If we do, we miss key opportunities to grow and develop ourselves in business and education and in our personal and business relationships. But it's okay to cherish happy, loving memories and call upon them when life is difficult or we're experiencing a crisis.

Life unfolds moment by moment. We generally let the present slip away, allowing time to rush past unobserved. We squander the precious seconds of our lives as we worry about the future and ruminate about the past.

Yes, we must mandate a vision for where we want to go and take ownership of where we currently are, but we can't neglect the present. It is here to help develop and mold us into being the best of ourselves.

Twenty years from now, once you have arrived at your goal—or maybe you'll just be *close* to your goal, because if you're ambitious like I am, there will always be another higher goal to pursue—you'll look back on your life and wish you had stopped and been present for all the wonderful things that took place.

THINGS YOU CAN TACKLE NOW TO ENSURE YOU ARE DOING YOUR BEST

1. Review and analyze. Consider how you've been trying to improve. Examine what you've done wrong and what you've done right. I've found that there are always ways I can improve no matter what area of life I'm tackling. When you continually review and analyze, you will always get new and different signals on how to get a better result.

2. Passion. Passion is the fuel for greatness. Find me a champion, someone who is the best at his or her craft, who isn't passionate. I can almost guarantee that you won't be able to give me more than one name. Evaluate what you've been doing and ask yourself if you're truly passionate about it. Without passion, your outcome will be so-so. Ignite that passion now!

3. Be the solution. Sometimes one of the biggest barriers standing in the way of achievement is yourself. Don't become the problem. That old saying "If you keep on getting what you're getting, it's because you keep on doing what you're doing" is apropos. You may be your own worst enemy. I certainly was when I wallowed in self-pity over some failure. Pick yourself up off the floor, and get to work doing your best.

4. Practice, practice, practice. No matter what you want to achieve, I can think of no better advice than practice, practice, practice. Strive to be a master of your craft. It will help you get to where you want to go every single time. It may not happen for you immediately, but eventually it will.

5. Surpass other people's expectations. Don't just meet other people's expectations; set out to surpass them. Not many people will ever set high expectations for your life, so aiming to just meet them will never get you to where you want to go. The way to ensure that you are doing your best to surpass expectations is to continually push yourself and work harder than ever before. As long as you're just doing what you've always done, you'll continue to get the same results and never get better. Set the bar of expectation high, and aim to surpass it.

Sometimes we may not give our best at work or in school until a problem arises. We wait to tell those we love how much they really mean to us, and then we regret it when they're gone. We forget about our most important values and priorities in life while we're rushing to earn a hefty paycheck or receive an extra bonus.

Regardless of our jobs and our socioeconomic status, we can benefit from learning how to live in the now and be as present as possible while still maintaining those long-term visions and plans.

Coach Hep certainly taught me that one of the major causes of unhappiness is to not appreciate what we already have and focus all our energy and effort toward what we don't have. As we age, some of our most precious assets will be the memories we created throughout the course of our lives. Don't forget to construct a life while you're busy making a living or building a business. There is no better time to start cherishing the present than right now. After all, not being present and choosing to not live life to the fullest just might be one of your biggest regrets while on your deathbed.

All these thoughts about living in the moment ran through my mind as I walked onto the playing field. I thought about Coach Hep and how he had prepped me for this moment when I was a Hoosier. I hoped I would make him proud once again.

I joined my teammates and coaches and had a great time on that first day of practice. I was both amazed and surprised at how much mental work was required when playing ball at the NFL level. But I was committed. Living in the now. Practicing my GBT as Coach Hep had taught me. And I was willing to do the work and whatever else was required of me.

In college, it's imperative to incorporate intense mental work into your sport, and you need to know the game of football very well, especially in a conference like the Big Ten. But the NFL was on another level altogether. It was overwhelming, to say the least. *Coach Hep, are you sure I can do this? Am I ready for this?*

I felt like his answer was a resounding yes!

After the first practice, we rookies understood how hard the mental workout was, as well as the physical one. We were given a quick half-hour lunch break to inhale our food, and then we were required to attend individual "position" meetings where we would watch videos of that day's practice to assess how well we did. There was no free time to dawdle.

Ten minutes into watching the first video, I cringed. I realized that I didn't do that well in practice from a *mental* standpoint. I was out of place often and missed a lot of called plays that were supposed to be executed by me. Although

I was a rookie and it was my first day of learning the new playbook, that was no excuse. I was now a professional. A member of the NFL. There was no room for error.

TACKLE THIS TODAY

Write your own playbook for a personal, a professional, or an educational goal and study it daily.

When you're an undrafted free agent, every single rep and practice is practically the Super Bowl for you. It's your time to shine and show that you belong right where you are with the big boys. Watching that video was brutal. I believed I had a great first practice and that I was off to a phenomenal start, and then boom! For one whole hour, I sat in front of the projector screen as the coach corrected my plays and told me, "You're not in place, Matt. Oh, look at that! You're too slow on that play. What happened there? Hell, you're not in control half the time."

My face burned with shame.

Generally, I'm great at receiving coaching tips and critiques. In fact, I had always welcomed them. I've had some extremely tough coaches over the years, but this particular moment was probably the toughest because I knew the magnitude of it. It was do or die for me. It was perform now or get cut.

That night after dinner, I returned to the hotel where all of us rookies were staying. I went into my room and lay down on my bed, staring at the ceiling. My roommate wasn't there, and I had some time to be alone. I questioned myself as I generally did. *Do I have what it takes to excel at the NFL level? Am I just fooling myself?*

I was completely overreacting, but my worries motivated me to study my playbook for nearly two more hours before I retired that night. My career was at stake.

The following day started bright and early at 6:00 A.M. It was day two of the rookie minicamp.

From the moment I crawled out of bed, I worked on my mind-set. I meditated for twenty minutes and spent some much-needed time in solitude. Then I visualized exactly how I wanted my day to go. I pictured excelling in the weight room and on the field during the plays I was going to execute at practice.

After surviving day one and studying the playbook for hours the previous night, my mental errors on the field were minimal. I was not perfect by any means, but I felt more at ease and more under control after the meditation, visualization, and solitude.

The one thing I quickly started to understand about the NFL and the pro game in general was that every little thing—how you lined up, the angles you took, and obviously how much you prepared—mattered more than it had while playing football in college.

I always used to get asked—and still do to this day— what is the major difference between college football and the NFL? My answer is always the same. "The game, as a whole, is much faster and every little detail matters."

In college, you can *mostly* get away with talent alone, but that doesn't happen too often in the NFL. Everyone at the NFL level is talented and one of the best at his position, or he wouldn't be there.

Watching day two's video sessions went much better than the first day. The coaches didn't correct me as much. Now and then, I'd even see one of them smile. I breathed easier. Sure, I still had a lot to accomplish to get where I wanted to be, but overall, I felt good about my second day as a Chicago Bear.

Dan LeFevour, one of my greatest childhood friends, was my roommate at the rookie minicamp. This meant a lot to me. Dan and I had played together on the Downers Grove Panthers junior football team when I was thirteen. Dan had an awesome career at Central Michigan University and was drafted by the Chicago Bears in the sixth round of the 2010 NFL Draft. It was such an incredible experience to have a friend at the minicamp, fighting for his childhood dream like I was.

The night before our last day of minicamp, Dan and I stayed up for an hour talking about how far we'd come. "How do you think you're doing?" Dan asked me.

"I gotta say the first day was rough," I admitted. "It was all those little things that I took for granted in college football, ya know?"

"Yeah, I wasn't prepared for all the mental workouts they've been giving us, but I think it's really helping overall."

"Me, too. I remember Coach Hep talking about mental conditioning—how we have to keep our minds in the right mind-set—but the NFL seems to take it to a whole new level."

We discussed our highs and lows of the journey up to this point. Having Dan right beside me enriched my experience and time even more.

The last day of rookie minicamp was by far my favorite of the three days at the Bears' headquarters. I was flying around, making plays, and feeling more confident in my abilities than I had felt in a long time.

The highlight of the last practice came when we had 7 on 7 against the offense and I made an interception and ran it back for a touchdown. That was just what I needed to make a good impression on the coaches and owners who were there watching. I was elated and pumped about that day's performance. I couldn't wait to get home and tell my family about the minicamp. I would have one month until the organized team activities (OTAs) started.

After practice concluded, television, newspaper, and magazine reporters lined up to interview me. In college, I used to have interviews and get swarmed by the media almost every day, especially toward the end of my junior and senior years, but this felt weird because it was the first time I stood in front of the media as an NFL professional football player.

"How did you feel that night when your name didn't get called in the draft?" one female TV reporter asked.

"How does it feel coming to play for a well-respected defensive powerhouse like the Bears, who produced Hall of Fame linebackers such as Mike Singletary and Dick Butkus?" another reporter asked.

"How does it feel to play with the probable future Hall of Famer Brian Urlacher, who's currently on the team with you?" a third one asked.

They lobbed question after question at me. I acted like it was just another interview and no big deal for me. But truth be told, that moment, with all the reporters swarming around me, gave me a special feeling. One that is really hard to describe in words. Kind of like, *I have arrived.* Imagine having a dream since you were a little kid and then eventually getting the opportunity to *live that dream.* That was how I felt.

"I'm very blessed and thankful that the Chicago Bears took a chance on me, selecting me as a free agent," I said. I didn't mention the fact that I still had a major chip on my shoulder from not getting drafted.

The following day, I woke up with twenty or so text messages from friends telling me that they saw my interview on television and that they were ecstatic about what Head Coach Lovie Smith said regarding my amazing athleticism.

I hadn't seen the video of this interview yet, so I grabbed my computer and logged on. Feeling blessed, I checked my e-mail and saw that a friend had sent me a link to the interview.

At the moment, I honestly didn't even care to watch my own interview. I just wanted to see what Lovie had to say. I must admit, it was awesome to hear my head coach—the man I had watched lead the Bears to play in the 2007 Super Bowl against the Indianapolis Colts—say great things about me. I have never been the type who goes fishing for compliments, and I have never needed another person to acknowledge that I did a great job. But every now and then it's nice to hear encouragement from your leader. It was simply the best.

Coach Lovie didn't say anything miraculous or even hint if I would make the team or not. He just reinforced the fact that I had the physical makeup and what it took to perform and succeed in this league. At the end of the interview he *did* say that it was all up to me whether I lived up to that potential. I couldn't agree more. It was up to me and me only.

We had a good amount of time off until we started back up with OTAs, where the whole team would work out together, practicing on the field and studying videos of our performances.

Every minute of every day during this time, I tried to do something to improve myself and fully prepare for the OTAs so I could stand out and solidify my chances of making this roster. I planned to make a good impression on all the veterans and coaches.

I kept Coach Hep's motto with me: "GBT—Get Better Today." And seven days a week, I worked on my craft, ate healthy, took care of my body, and meditated on and visualized the ideal outcome that I wanted.

TACKLE THIS TODAY

Do you have a mentor in school or in business to help guide and teach you? Take a look around you. Whom do you admire? Whom do you aspire to be like? Do you listen to others who could help you, or do you think you already know it all? What can you learn from others today?

Each head coach of every NFL team has different rules on who reports to what, and we had only a couple of veterans at our minicamp, so I was very eager to meet all of them, *especially* the linebackers.

When it was finally time to report to the OTAs, the first group of veteran teammates in my linebacker room were Brian Urlacher, Lance Briggs, Hunter Hillenmeyer, Nick Roach, Pisa Tinoisamoa, and Tim Shaw. It was a great group of guys, and I was fortunate to have them not only as teammates but as mentors. Each and every one of them took the time to ask me how I was doing. "Don't hesitate to let us know if you need any help with anything," they told me.

As a linebacker in college, I paid close attention to a select few linebackers, and Brian Urlacher was one of them. I loved his tenacity on the football field, but more important, I admired his speed and ability to make plays all over the field. I was a huge fan of Brian's, and he was one guy who definitely did not fail to impress. He took time out of his day to speak with me and always asked if I needed any help with the playbook.

I was also extremely appreciative of fellow Pro Bowl linebacker Lance Briggs. Brian and Lance, the stars on the team, were two of the best players and also the hardest working and most respected. They walked the walk in everything they did.

I heard stories from other friends who were on teams all around the NFL, and most of them had some not-so-nice things to say about the veterans. I was blessed that I didn't have to join in on those kinds of stories.

The OTAs went well and acclimated me on a deeper level—mind, body, and soul. Minicamp was crucial and I learned a lot, but nothing was more beneficial than being on the practice field with the veterans. We installed new defensive packages, competed against the offense, and watched many videos to mentally prepare for training camp, which was right around the corner.

Training camp happened each and every year like clockwork, right in the heat of summer with many days logging record temperatures. Yes, it meant the football season was officially under way and that the excitement of the season was upon us, but NFL training camp was a total grind from sunup to sundown, and it was, by far, the most dreaded and brutal part about football at this level.

We were up before sunrise and worked late into the evenings, had curfews and minimal breaks, and were completely shut off to the outside world for nearly a whole month. Our entire focus was on football. It was necessary, though, being an extremely pivotal moment for all football teams to prepare for a championship season.

During our time off between OTAs and training camp, I pushed myself hard and worked like never before.

Even though I performed well in the OTAs and slowly started to receive respect from some of the veterans, I knew that the only way for an undrafted free agent to make an NFL team was to have a terrific training camp and preseason, and that was exactly what I intended to do.

THE PHYSICAL AND MENTAL WORKOUT

In addition to practicing on the field with the veterans, I worked out on my own at the gym in Chicago when I was home. While training there on Saturdays, I noticed another NFL player who trained at the same time I did. It was Mike Neal, who had played college football at our biggest rival, Purdue. He had been a second-round selection by the Green Bay Packers in April. Mike had reached out to me after the Indiana-Purdue game when we were in college and told me that he liked my game.

Mike and I both wanted to improve in the weight room, so we started working out together and built a friendship. We often talked about the Big Ten Conference and what it was like playing at our respective schools. We analyzed the other teams, discussed where we were training, and compared our situations when we had to transition from college football to the NFL.

We both had a real desire to get *better* even when we were off the field. Coach Hep had thoroughly drilled GBT into my mind.

Mike and I took our training very seriously, but we joked with each other a lot. He said I was hard on him, but I just laughed about it. We went to rival colleges and now played on rival NFL teams, so we had a natural banter.

"Hey, meathead." Neal laughed. "Can you give a brother a break here? I mean, we're not training for the Olympics." He looked at the heavy weights and sighed, then took a deep breath and began.

Neal was referring to the way I pushed him through the workouts. I had a drive to be the best at anything I attempted, including weight lifting. I had to admit, I readily pushed others. But he pushed me, as well.

"You know, meathead, I don't know anyone else who would do these ass-kickin' workouts but you."

"Well, you make it look easy," I told him. "You're freakish with the amount of weight you can lift."

"I'm nowhere near as strong as you," Neal said.

But I knew he was much tougher and stronger than I was.

One time we were working out with Kevin Kasper, a former Iowa and NFL wide receiver. It was one of Mike's first times working out with us. Mike complained how hurt he was and that his chest was sore. We began some difficult push-ups, and I expected Mike would just halfway do them. But he crushed them.

I looked at Mike like he was crazy. From what I had seen, he'd flown through the push-ups like they were child's play. "Where did that come from? I thought you were sore and couldn't do much today."

"I don't know where that little bit of energy came from," Mike said. "I don't think I have anything else left today. My arms are hurting, and I can't really feel my hands."

I knew that Neal didn't know how strong he was until he tried it. In fact, he was so strong that people nicknamed him Incredible Hulk. "You're not quitting on me," I told him. "We're just getting started."

We motivated each other even when we were sore, injured, and tired. We talked almost every other day and shared books, workout tips, and motivational suggestions. Mike and I helped each other stay on course physically when we trained. But one of the most important things we did was help each other with our *mental workouts*. Transitioning to the NFL is mentally tough. As both Neal and I continued in training camp, we realized that survival was more about the mental than the physical. Every player—whether he's a rookie, a journeyman, an established veteran, or a marquee free-agent acquisition—faces mental challenges heading into a six-week endeavor that requires tremendous levels of preparation, concentration, focus, and perseverance.

TACKLE THIS TODAY

It helps to have a buddy to study with, work out in the gym with, discuss business ideas with, and just be your confidant. We are not meant to go through this life without friends, family, or loved ones. Do you have someone you can work with? Brainstorm with? When you face a challenge, is there anyone to help you?

The coaches defined mental toughness as the ability to maintain the focus and determination to complete a course of action despite difficulty or consequences—to never quit, period. To many athletes and coaches, it's an innate quality that can't be trained. Some people think that mental toughness is something you're born with or develop very early in life due to your surroundings.

I believe my father and Grampa Dee instilled this mental toughness in me at an early age. But I believe anyone—at any time—can improve his performance, tolerance, patience, focus, and concentration, just as anyone can get bigger, leaner, or better educated.

One day Neal and I sat down on the bench after lifting, wiping the sweat off our faces, and rested. "I'm not gonna lie. That was tough," I said.

"Yeah, but you're a beast. You make it look easy."

"It's not easy. It's just hard work."

"You know what? The most difficult part of this whole transition to the NFL is mental. It's the time commitment, the study of the game, and the stuff we have to know. I think that being a rookie, you can get a little bogged down in it all."

"I know. There's just a lot going on. But you were a second-round selection. I feel like I have more to prove being a free agent. Everyone's watching my performance to see how I play."

"Nah, that's not true," said Neal. "I mean, sure, everyone's watching how you play, but they watch all of us. I admit being a draft pick carries a lot of hype, but everyone has to earn his keep."

"It's hard especially when the coaches yell even when we feel like we're doing things the right way." I felt like they were always yelling at me to do something a different way, but I believed it helped me in the long run.

Neal and I motivated each other mentally and physically. Things like text messages, phone calls, and even Twitter helped us keep going when things got tough. People don't realize that the little things can give you big encouragement. When it came down to it, Neal and I both loved to work hard physically and mentally in the weight room and on the football field. I'm grateful for his friendship. He made the mental and physical workouts bearable. He also just finished his sixth season as a veteran Green Bay Packer.

THINGS YOU CAN TACKLE NOW TO ACHIEVE A MENTAL WORKOUT

1. Laser-focus. It's important to be able to shut out the world on a regular basis and laser-focus on the job at hand. Turn off your smartphones and all social media for at least twenty minutes a day. You can take a walk or simply sit somewhere quietly and just breathe...relax. Some people call this mindfulness meditation. When your thoughts begin to wander, gently pull them back. When that work meeting pops into your head, push it out and focus on your breathing. When you start mentally planning your next workout, return to your breathing. This can have dramatic results and will help you in your work and activities toward achieving your dreams.

2. Exercise. I know we're discussing the mental here, but honestly, doing something physical can really pay off for your mental work. Lifting weights and cardio are two of the best methods to strengthen working memory and intelligence. The trick, however, is to keep pushing yourself, just like Neal and I pushed each other during our workouts to increase the intensity. If you work out at the level you've always done—like running a mile, for example—then you'll stay where you are mentally. You have to push yourself a little past your limit to expand the mind.

3. Study. Whatever you're pursuing, study it. For me, it was the playbook. I had to study it inside and out. After practices I also studied the videos of my and other teammates' performances. So, no matter what you're pursuing, study it by reading books about it, watching videos about it, and joining others to discuss it. This builds up your knowledge of the sport or whatever it is you're interested in. It builds your mental strength.

––––––––––––

While training, I had to continually tell myself that I hadn't arrived yet. I had seen it play out all too often when someone thought they had "made it" and suddenly stopped putting in the required work and sacrifice to be the absolute best. Whether it was the old drug friends reaching out to tempt me in high school, people in the local community treating me like a superstar in college, or young ladies viewing me in a different way just because I was temporarily a Chicago Bear, every day I had to block out the noise and hype and give it my all.

Many people allow the assumptions of others and the noise from the outside world to get into their heads, which directly affects their performance and how they go about their everyday lives and business. I have seen it a thousand times. Someone will achieve a little bit of success, and they let their ego swell up, majorly disrupting their potential to perform at a high level on a consistent basis. So I remained humble. Even though it was awesome to be treated well and to get all that attention, I had to constantly remind myself that I was still an undrafted player who had a long and difficult road ahead.

Once training camp came back around, even though I hated it with all my heart, I treated every meeting, practice, and interaction with other teammates and coaches as business.

However, I worried that I wasn't measuring up to the others. The coaches encouraged us to focus on our own performance rather than everyone else's, and it was one of the best pieces of advice a leader could give us players who were fighting for our careers. Still, the pressure to outdo the competition could force even the most confident player to question his ability.

Just like Neal and I had discussed, I had to concentrate on my mental game. Every spare minute between meetings or practice, I studied my playbook, striving to refine my game and increase my chances to make the team. One of the best ways for me to break all odds was to contribute in a major way on special teams. This was where most rookies made their living. It was where most had the opportunity to solidify their chances for adding value to an NFL team.

Even though I was laser-focused on the job at hand and on making this team, I couldn't help but tear up at times when reflecting on my journey. I had barely escaped another horrible life altogether. I recalled everything from when I was a sixteen-year-old drug addict to my college football days at Indiana University. I now wanted to be a Chicago Bear more than anything. I wanted it for my parents and grandparents, who had done everything possible to not only save my life but help me achieve my dream of playing a game I absolutely loved. My parents had traveled to every single football game I ever played, from my Pop Warner days to Indiana. Whether it was the four-hour drive to Bloomington, Indiana, or nine hours to Penn State, they were there, each wearing my jersey, cheering me on. They sacrificed more than I could ever repay them for. The Chicago Bears was their favorite team.

This was surely their ultimate dream for me as well. So few people were ever given this opportunity. I wanted to make them proud of me.

Tears welled in my eyes when I thought of how blessed I had been up to this point. I could easily be dead or in prison like my guidance counselor had predicted when I was sixteen.

I had many angels, including Coach Hep, who helped me and guided me. I had Neal, my best bud, and my teammates, along with the emotional support from my family. And that made all the difference.

YOUR OWN PERSONAL GAME PLAN
TO PUT INTO ACTION

1. Live in the now. Regardless of where you may be in your life, whether it's a time of failure and distress or a time of unbelievable success, don't forget to live in the now. Be as present as possible. All too often, we let our ambition and desire get in the way of enjoying life today. Living in the moment doesn't mean completely forgetting about the past and the future; it means not allowing the past or the future to control the present. I can honestly say that one of the things I am most proud of during my time in the NFL was being present every single moment and taking it all in. People who rush, rush, rush toward their future often forget about what they're doing right now. Time goes quickly, and if you don't stop and enjoy what's occurring, at the end of your life you'll end up wondering what happened.

2. Do the work. Prepare like no one else. Do the work others aren't willing to do. Being around future Hall of Famers and seeing up close and personal what it really took to excel was eye-opening. I immediately noticed the ridiculous amount of preparation and hard work that was required. Sure, many people would love to have the glory and accolades of becoming a Hall of Famer, but how many would actually do the work to obtain it? That is the question. Start today. Dedicate yourself from this day forward to prepare to be the best you can be at whatever it is you want to do. Study, research, practice, prepare. It's never *enough* to just do what's required. If you truly want to be great and never let another failure or hardship dictate what's in store for you, prepare like your life depends on it, because it does. The better prepared you are, the better you'll be able to manage all the roadblocks that life will throw your way. Great preparation breeds great performance.

3. Celebrate every day. There is power in celebrating everything—especially the *small* daily wins. When I broke down and cried tears of joy that night thinking about how blessed I was to have the opportunity of a lifetime to play for the Chicago Bears, it boosted my confidence tremendously, gave me deep satisfaction, and, most important, made me feel great. Make it a personal habit right now to start celebrating everything in your life. Just because you haven't reached one of your main goals yet doesn't mean you can't have fun and capitalize on where you currently are. One good way to get in the habit is by recording your small daily wins in a journal. I use a Moleskine notebook, and at the end of each day I write down five wins for that specific day. It doesn't matter how bad my overall day was or what happened, I force myself to jot down five positive things. It puts me in a positive state of mind before I go to bed and builds momentum for the following day. Whether big, medium, or small, it doesn't matter. Celebrate those wins!

Chapter Seven

THE SUPER BOWL

What seem to us bitter trials are often blessings in disguise.

—*Oscar Wilde*

This might as well have been my Super Bowl. I could smell the freshness of the wet dirt and the long grass. Far off in the distance, I could hear the din of fans screaming, cheering us on. There was an iron, salty taste in my mouth. This was where I belonged.

This game was a preseason matchup against the San Diego Chargers out in beautiful California. For anyone unfamiliar with the NFL, preseason games take place before the start of the regular season. Each NFL team has only fifty-three spots available when the regular season comes around. This makes the preseason über-important for the rookies and undrafted free agents around the league.

Leading up to our game with San Diego, I knew I would get a good amount of playing time, because the normal starters were in for only ten to fifteen plays. My coach wanted to see how I would do in a live game situation. To me, this game was everything I had been working for my entire life.

I was off to a good start, recording three tackles and a tackle for loss. Besides missing a sack opportunity, I thought I was playing well. I was pumped. Elated to be doing what I had always dreamed of doing. Life simply couldn't get any better.

Late in the second quarter with four minutes left to go before halftime, a big Chargers offensive lineman started chopping at my legs. His 280-pound bulk came down hard across my leg, and my ankle was badly tangled up under this mountain of a man.

When I attempted to stand, I knew that what seemed to be a routine moment in the game was not routine at all for me. A sharp pain stabbed through my entire leg. I felt sick as the searing pain became progressively worse by the second. In fact, the pain was so intense, I thought I might faint at any moment.

I focused with every fiber in my being. Getting beyond this was my goal. *Just get back to the team. C'mon, keep moving.* Walking to the huddle, I assessed the situation and figured I would continue playing, as there were only a few minutes left before halftime.

After the second quarter, I staggered to the locker room, immediately took off my shoulder pads and helmet, and called for the medical trainers to inspect my swollen ankle.

"It's just sprained," they insisted, based on the simple tests they performed on the spot.

It's a painful sprain but just a sprain. I can handle a sprain!

I desperately wanted to continue playing, as I knew it was vital for me to be out on the field to display my skills as a rookie, so that was exactly what I did. I took some pain medicine and headed back out to the field with the rest of my teammates when it was time to start the third quarter.

In the short term, stress and the chemical reactions of medicine can be a powerful painkiller. When the brain senses a serious threat or a traumatic injury, it releases a veritable pharmacy of chemicals to alleviate the pain. Called stress-induced analgesia, this reaction explains why people often don't feel pain immediately following an injury. It enables a soldier in battle, or, for that matter, a deer trying to outrun a mountain lion after escaping from its claws, to focus on survival rather than pain. Some soldiers who are hit by enemy fire don't even realize they've been injured until the battle is over.

Interestingly enough, the painkillers released by the body during stress are very similar to chemicals found in illicit drugs. In addition to blocking pain, these chemicals trigger the release of dopamine, a compound that provides feelings of pleasure. Adrenaline always blocked out the minor hurts when I played, and that was exactly what happened during the game. I fought through the pain and tried my best to ignore it. Fortunately, the medicine began to kick in, which helped to an extent.

I finished the game with six tackles and a tackle for loss. I was satisfied with my performance, but as a competitor, I always expected more from myself. However, on this day, my performance was not first and foremost on my mind. All I could think about was how excruciating the pain was becoming in my ankle and leg. And I was shocked at the all-too-real possibility of how devastating this could be for me and for everyone else who was counting on me in my football career.

We flew back to Chicago around 1:00 A.M. When I made it home, I immediately got some ice and propped my foot up to keep it elevated all night. But sleep escaped me. I couldn't relax long enough to fall asleep until later the next evening. The pain, the fear, the feelings of being a failure, consumed me.

That next day, I went to the Chicago Bears medical facility at 1:00 P.M. for treatment on my ankle. The physicians didn't say much, but from their gloomy demeanor and evasive comments, I suspected the worst. We scheduled an appointment for an MRI with an orthopedic specialist the next week. Oh, how I dreaded seeing him! In my heart, I knew it wouldn't be good news.

TACKLE THIS TODAY

If something happens to your Plan A, do you have a Plan B in place? Think about it. What would you do if your dreams all of a sudden fell apart?

While I waited to see the specialist, I had an extremely hard time sleeping and focusing in team meetings. I was consumed with anxiety and fear, and I slid into the deepest depths of darkness. My life was shattering; my dreams and goals were like shards of glass before me. I had no Plan B in place.

It has been my experience that most athletes are often ill prepared, if not left completely in the dark, when it comes to the emotional and psychological aspects of sustaining an injury and the subsequent recovery. It was traumatic for me and signaled the end of my career and my dreams and goals.

I didn't go out on the field for practice that week. I was told to stay off my leg so I wouldn't injure my ankle more severely. Instead, I lay there in my bed, stewing in my own misery.

When I went to see the specialist, the news I was praying *not to hear* was all-consuming. I didn't want to hear the word *sorry*. I didn't want to hear any reluctance at all. But the pain in my leg was already telling me the exact news that I was dreading.

"Matt, sorry to tell you this," said the orthopedic specialist, "but a piece of bone in your left ankle was completely torn off."

"What?" My gut seized up.

He showed me the results of the scan and pointed out the broken bone.

"How long will I be out?" I asked, trying to stay calm.

"Four to six months." He had a hard time looking me in the eye. He knew what this meant for me professionally. Four to six months was an entire season in the NFL. That was an eternity.

I was devastated. Heartbroken. I was unable to breathe, and I felt as if he had just punched me right in the gut. I sat in silence, not knowing what to do next. As an NFL rookie, a four- to six-month recovery could easily mean the end of your career. A million thoughts and emotions raced through my mind. All of them were focused on despair, anguish, and failure.

"Thank you, Doc." It was barely a whisper.

I was numb, completely in a daze, as I slowly went back to my car, hopping along on my good leg, with my medical report in hand. *I must return to the Chicago Bears facility.* I had to show them the MRI results and face the truth.

As word spread about my diagnosis, I knew the front office would have a decision to make. Either keep me on the roster and waste salary space or reach an injury settlement, which would free up some room for them to make another transaction with a rookie.

Two days later, Lovie Smith, who was the head coach of the Bears at the time, made a decision. "This is the tough part of this business, but we will be letting you go with an injury settlement. You had an outstanding camp, and we believe here that you have what it takes to be a great player in this league."

I looked at him blankly. In my mind, I screamed and cursed his decision. *What the hell am I going to do? Do you know how hard I worked for this? What am I going to tell my family? They were so proud of me.* I felt sick. But I understood the decision. *The NFL is a business. I knew this coming in. It's just so much harder to accept coming out.*

Outwardly, I was professional. "All right, I understand." And because I was raised to be a gentleman, I added, "Thank you very much for this."

Smith shook my hand and patted me on the back. "Good luck to you, Matt. I know you will do well."

Where? Recovering in my boot? What could I possibly do now that I didn't have a team? What if I had accepted the offer from the Texans or Falcons? I bet I'd still be playing. I had failed. My dreams of being an NFL player and having a successful life and wonderful career had just bottomed out. I was already a has-been.

I remembered a famous quote from Mike Tyson that said it all: "Everyone has a plan until they get punched in the face." It reminded me that we all have glorious and magnificent plans, but once we experience a major setback or failure, we have no clue how to respond or move forward. It felt like I now belonged to that group of the population that ends up helplessly down for the count rather than fighting back.

Any highly successful person—such as an athlete, an entrepreneur, a parent, a manager, a politician, or a salesperson—has also experienced a great deal of failure. The people at the top, the game changers, have all had a ridiculous amount of *unsuccessful* years before any of their successful years became known to the public.

At the time, though, I couldn't focus on those people who had failed many times before they succeeded. All I could do was stumble out to the car that was waiting to take me back to the facility and try my best not to think about the injury.

THINGS YOU CAN TACKLE NOW TO RECOVER FROM A CRUSHED DREAM

1. Face the facts. If something has crushed your dream, do you find that you are in denial? I wasn't really in denial—I didn't think there was life after the NFL, so I hadn't even reached the point of denial yet—but I was in a death spiral. I believed if I couldn't play football, then life as I knew it was over. If you're in denial about a crushed dream, or if you're succumbing to the "death" feeling where demons roam and you believe that nothing matters in life anymore, you need to face the facts. We all have to look at those facts objectively and analyze our next move, no matter how painful it is.

2. Don't overanalyze. We might overanalyze when something happens to crush our dream. We might worry ourselves to death, wondering what we're going to do. We might tell ourselves it's a nightmare and that tomorrow we'll wake up and things will be okay. Don't overthink things. Give yourself time to absorb the reality of the situation, and don't rush into "fixing" things.

3. Surrender. Simply surrender this to a higher power. You can't change what has happened, but you can change how you react to it. The Beatles song "Tomorrow Never Knows" suggests that we meditate to try to find meaning within ourselves. This is perfect advice; since we can't change the situation, we may as well turn off our minds and surrender to it. It is then that the solutions will surface. Just like long walks and meditation can give you peace of mind and answers to questions that bother you, so can the surrender of pain. Of course, this is easier said than done, and I certainly didn't do this at the time.

4. Acceptance. Surrendering to the situation is similar to acceptance. And mind you, I did not accept my situation well at all. I kept asking myself, *What if I had tackled differently on that play? What if I had chosen a different team's offer?* I realize now more than ever that acceptance is crucial to forgiving yourself and moving on. Leave all the what-ifs behind. I had to get rid of them and accept my circumstances before I could go forward.

This injury was the biggest failure of my life. A calamity of epic proportions. In my early twenties, I had already failed plenty. But this was beyond anything I ever thought possible. I was at rock bottom, and my life had just imploded. My dreams were crushed, and I was staggered and embarrassed. Lost. Depressed. I was a failure, and the whole world knew it because *I was Matt Mayberry*, an NFL linebacker for the Chicago Bears. Only now, I wasn't.

At first, I certainly didn't see any hope—much less a blessing or a gift for me—in this. I tried to take comfort by remembering what Coach Hep had told me. "You *will excel* on the field and probably have the chance to play in the NFL someday, but you will become more successful *outside* of football than you ever are in football."

It was hard to believe in myself at the moment. It was hard to believe what Coach Hep had told me. It was hard to believe I would ever be successful at anything ever again.

YOUR OWN PERSONAL GAME PLAN TO PUT INTO ACTION

1. Power through. There will be plenty of times throughout your journey when the going will get tough and you will feel like you can't continue. However, when you fight through the temporary pain, no matter how bad it may physically and mentally hurt, and keep moving forward, you will eventually be victorious. You must leave your comfort zone and get uncomfortable every single day of your life. Not sometimes but every day. It might be overcoming the fear that has been holding you back, operating on minimal sleep while spearheading a start-up, or putting in long hours year after year. That night when I played on my broken ankle, I realized how much fight is within people who want something passionately. Even though I shouldn't have continued to play, I powered through, because that was how bad I wanted it. I was willing to do whatever it took, and so should you. *Power through and fight for your dream!*

2. **Control what you can control.** Oftentimes, when we experience a major setback or failure, we start focusing on every little thing beyond our control. When you put all your energy and effort into controlling what you can actually control, not only do you increase the chances of your situation improving, but you also liberate yourself from an enormous amount of stress. It's a waste of energy to worry about those things you can't control. I made my life much worse, because one of the first things I did was focus on everything that was beyond my control. The next time a failure, adversity, or a setback occurs in your life, concentrate and focus on what you can control in that exact moment.

3. **Focus on the positive.** There are three areas you should focus on when failure or hardship strikes. It's no easy task, because when something goes wrong, it's easy to become negative, and that will prohibit you from performing at a high level. If you can focus on the positive, it will help you in all areas of your life. Here are three areas to which you should turn your focus, *especially* when life throws you curveballs:

   1) **Mind-set, your perception of yourself.** How do you perceive yourself? Do you constantly criticize your every

move and thought? Don't you realize that you can't be great if you don't think you're great? You have to own it. You must already have this in your mind-set before you become great in reality. The same goes for when adversity strikes. Your perception of yourself matters, because this affects your thoughts, and these thoughts will lead us to victory or continual defeat over and over again. One of the main reasons why positive thinking has caught a bad rap over the years is because some people will tell you to *think positive* and stop there. Positive thinking alone does no good. It has to be paired with action—*and massive action at that*. When that happens, phenomenal things manifest.

2) **Relationships.** Surround yourself with people who inspire you to be better. Befriend those who support you and believe in you. You don't need people who are negative and drain your energies, mooch off you, and take advantage of you. Positive, uplifting relationships serve as a springboard to your being more positive about your life in multiple ways.

3) **Expectations.** Failure can affect your expectations. It's hard to expect anything good to happen when you fail time after time. But if you don't expect something good, then you may not get it. What you visualize about yourself and expect to happen can come true. Create positive expectations by surrounding yourself with the best of people. When you do this, there won't be room for the negative.

Chapter Eight

I AM BROKEN

Turn your wounds into wisdom.

—Oprah Winfrey

If someone had really looked at me, they would have seen that my eyes were dim, with the light fading to blackness and not a spark of life. If they had peeked inside me, they would have seen shards of glass gouging my heart, breaking it into pieces. They would have seen a soul that had been trampled and crushed with nothing left but a trail of ashes in its wake.

Darkness had consumed me, and there was no opening for a tiny crack of light.

I am broken. Maybe I'll just kill myself. I said these words over and over. Not that I would have really done it, but dying seemed a lot easier than living. To not have to struggle anymore. To not have to try and prove myself anymore. Death seemed more peaceful. *Just let go, Matt,* a voice inside suggested.

It's a dark, dark world, and I'm so broken. That was exactly how I felt when I received the news that I wouldn't be playing

135

football for at least four to six months. I actually felt like I'd *never* be out on that football field again. I watched my dream of playing for the Chicago Bears, the hometown team I grew up loving so much, disappear right before my eyes.

Did I have any value to offer the world outside of my athletic ability? No. In my mind, I did not.

I suppose all of us are broken at different times in our lives. I know that I'm not the only person who has gone through something like this. People experience brokenness through illness, the loss of a job, the derailment of a dream, and the loss of loved ones. And while I didn't know it at that time, I have learned that we are all stronger, gentler, more resilient, more resourceful, and more beautiful than we imagine. The answers to our problems are never far away. Sometimes it can just take a while to get there.

I wonder how many people are broken right now. Do they ever become whole, or do they patch themselves up with bandages and continue on, always half broken while wearing the wounds and scars for the rest of their lives? I felt as though the wounds and scars were piling on my body, and I wasn't sure I would ever be whole again.

TACKLE THIS TODAY

Take a look at your heart. Is it broken? Please remember that not only will your heart mend, but it will also become larger, stronger, and more loving for the breaking.

Right after I received the news from the doctor, I was headed back to the team facility to pick up my luggage and other personal belongings I had stored there while at training camp. It was only a twenty-minute ride, but it felt like the longest of my life.

The trees blurred in greens and browns past the windshield. I barely noticed through the tears streaming down my face. It was like life was passing me by in a foggy haze. I had screwed up everything, and all I could think about were my failures, personal tragedies, and shortcomings. From my drug-addled past to the pain I had caused my family, to losing Coach Hep at Indiana, and then to top it all off, losing my opportunity to live my dream of being a Chicago Bear. *Let's face it. I'm a nobody. A has-been.* I was a complete wreck mentally, emotionally, physically, and spiritually.

I couldn't quite come to grips with, or even remotely understand, why my journey was filled with so many ups and downs. Why couldn't I achieve a childhood dream and continue being successful and making those closest to me proud of all the good that I was doing with my life? Why did these failures and tragedies keep happening to me? Was I doing something wrong?

Sure, I knew that many professional athletes got injured while playing the game. I wasn't the only one. It just seemed that way at the time.

I retraced my footsteps. I had kicked being a junkie at age sixteen and worked hard to become the best athlete I could. That paid off. I had received offers for a Division I scholarship from top universities after one of the darkest periods of my life. I chose Indiana University and enjoyed an award-winning football career at Indiana. I met Coach Hoeppner, one of my favorite people of all time who became a father figure, coach, mentor, leader, and friend. I faced tragedy and heartbreak when I lost Coach Hep to a brain tumor. Once again, I had to deal with loss and pain and pick myself up off the floor and survive. Then I was up for the NFL Draft. I wasn't drafted, which was a blow to my ego, but I finally got the chance to play for the Chicago Bears as a free agent. I was thrilled. And then I got seriously hurt during my debut against the San Diego Chargers. I mean, you've got to be kidding me.

I wanted to make something special out of my life, but every time I thought I was getting somewhere, I was thrown a curveball. I started to question my faith in God and feel sorry for myself.

TACKLE THIS TODAY

Are you wrestling with yourself at the moment? Have you been thrown a curveball? If so, what are you doing about it?

Of course, I later realized that everyone goes through ups and downs. Tragedies and failures do not discriminate. It doesn't matter if one is rich, poor, popular, young, old, or whatever. Life is going to knock you down, and depending on how you react, it can make or break you. I was not the first person to get hurt playing a sport I loved, but at that young age, I felt that way. I felt as if life was determined to knock me down at every turn.

I retrieved all of my belongings at the facility. As I drove home, I thought about my living situation. I didn't have my own apartment, because the team stayed in dorms at Olivet Nazarene University. It was standard protocol for the Chicago Bears to stay there when they were training. Naturally, I hadn't planned on renting an apartment until I knew for sure I was going to make the team. And it was a good thing I hadn't.

Going back to live at my parents' house after being on my own in college and playing in the NFL was a reality check. I was no longer a big-time athlete but just a regular guy. All of a sudden, I'd have to check in with my parents and tell them where I was going and when I'd be coming home.

I had no job, no money, no career, nothing.

Depressed, feeling sorry for myself, and counting all my failures, tragedies, and struggles, I seriously started to think about how lovely it would be to just be dead. To end my life in the blink of an eye and have the pain disappear. To let Death wrap me in its arms and take me away from it all. I've heard people say that dying was easy; it's living that's the hard thing. And I believed it.

I wasn't necessarily contemplating suicide or thinking of a master plan about how I was going to take my own life, but for quite some time, I thought about how lovely it would be to just be dead. So serene.

I was sick and tired of working hard, trying my best, and failing. I was completely sick and tired of overcoming one major hurdle after another, only to get knocked back down.

TACKLE THIS TODAY

We all get knocked down in life. We fail. And the most successful people have probably failed the most. What about you? How many times have you failed at something you desperately wanted? And what did you do about it?

My mother was home when I got there. I dragged everything inside and lugged it upstairs to my room without saying a word to her. I wanted to be left alone.

My father got home from work around 5:45 P.M. I heard him come in the front door. "Honey, I'm home!" he yelled to her. "I'm going to take a shower."

"Okay, dear," my mom called out.

Dad headed upstairs to the bathroom.

I doubted he knew I was home. I stayed quiet and lay on my bed, wondering how I was going to face them.

Then I heard Dad go downstairs to watch the evening news. I had no desire to get off the bed or do anything.

An hour later, the aroma of basil and garlic wafted through the air. It was a nostalgic smell, one that had crossed over from happy childhood memories. I had dreamed about my mom's home cooking all four years I was away at college. I used to bring my teammates home on the weekends during the off-season, and she would cook for us. Mom knew food was the way to my heart, and normally I'd be ravenous, but that night, I had no appetite. Food was depressing. Being home was depressing. Everything was depressing.

Mom had heard me come into the house, but she hadn't said anything to me yet. She probably thought I was home for a break. It wasn't long before she came up to my room, where my door was cracked open about an inch. She poked her head in. "Matt, dinner's ready, okay?"

"Sure," I said. I didn't move a muscle.

"What's wrong?" Mom opened my door wider and glanced at my suitcase and boxes that were strewn across the floor. I had the bedcovers over my legs and feet on the bed. I didn't want her to see my injured ankle. Not yet. I knew she could tell by my puffy eyes that something was wrong, but she didn't say anything about it. Instead, she acted as if everything was normal. "We'll be waiting for you at the dinner table. I made spaghetti."

I had no appetite. No desire for anything.

"C'mon down when you're ready." With that, she turned and went back downstairs. No doubt, she warned my dad that something was wrong. Very wrong.

I had to tell them what happened, so I rolled off the bed, put my foot into the walking boot that supported the injured ankle, and went downstairs. I shuffled my feet slowly to the dinner table with my head down. I didn't want them to see that I had been crying. I pulled out a chair and slumped into it.

Dad, Mom, and my brother, Gary, looked at me with questioning eyes. Of course they noticed the walking boot. There was no denying that I had been injured. But for a moment, no one said anything. It was so quiet that I worried they could hear the loud pounding of my heart. It felt as though a thousand drums were beating against it.

Finally, Dad spoke up. "Matt, um...is everything okay? Did you hurt your ankle at training camp?"

How could I tell them? They had invested so much money, time, and effort in helping me become a great athlete. I had let them down. I was such a big failure. "I didn't know how to tell you guys this, but I suffered an injury in the game... and—"

"Oh no, what happened?" Mom blurted out. I saw the worry in her eyes. She gave Dad a look.

"It seems like every time there's something good happening in my life, it all falls apart." I stared down at my plate, avoiding their eyes.

"Tell us what happened," Dad said. His voice was calm but strained.

I explained that a bone was completely torn off my ankle and that I would be out of football for roughly four to six months, and potentially longer depending on how well I healed and did in rehab.

"Oh, Matt," Mom said, "you'll be all right. This happens to a lot of players. You'll recover and get back in the game soon."

"We're here for you, son," Dad said. "We'll help you any way we can. You know that. And you're strong and physically fit. You'll be fine."

I shrugged.

My parents continued talking, letting me know that no matter what, they would help me recover and get strong again. All I heard was a blur of words slipping past me into the atmosphere. Similar to my NFL dreams. I wasn't listening. I was depressed. Broken. Too resolved that my life was over. There was no Plan B.

During the next few days, my parents saw how devastated I was. I had always taken things to heart. I put everything I have into something, and when I fail, it crushes me. Call it sensitivity or whatever you want; I just take things very seriously.

So my parents called in the big guns—Grampa Dee and Grandma, my dad's parents. My mother's parents were also important to me; it just seemed that Grampa Dee had been the most instrumental in encouraging me in sports and in life.

Grampa Dee and Grandma visited me during those two and a half weeks, but I barely left my room to see them. I loved them with all my heart, but I felt too depressed, too ashamed. That's what it was...*shame*.

Dad continually said, "Matt, you've been through rough times before and you pulled through. You're stronger than you think you are." My parents encouraged me, telling me I would be all right and I would have another chance to play football.

"This isn't a career-ending injury," Dad said. "It could have been so much worse. You could have sustained a brain injury or gotten paralyzed."

I knew that was true, but I was beyond listening to anything anyone had to say. I totally shut down. Doctors had told me I'd be out four to six months, and maybe more, and in the NFL, undrafted free agents have no time for injury. *If you can't play, you're gone.* Without the NFL, I had no identity.

From somewhere deep, deep inside my cold heart, I heard Coach Hep saying, "Football is *what* you do, Matt; it's not *who* you are."

I was too closed off to listen. I was drowning in the darkness, and the light was completely gone from my life.

Outwardly, I tried to act like I was okay to my parents, but I knew I was not okay.

Mom continued to cook all my favorite meals—anything and everything she could—to lift my spirits, but the food was tasteless to me.

Even Gary, who was busy playing baseball in high school, tried to talk to me, but he caught on pretty quickly that I wasn't in the right frame of mind, and he let me be.

For two and a half weeks, I hardly talked to any family members and definitely didn't talk to any of my friends. The media called, wanting to do interviews, but I refused. I was closed for business.

Mom suggested I go out with some friends, but I didn't. I received text messages, Facebook messages, Twitter messages, and phone calls left and right from old teammates, family members, and friends from high school and college. I also received letters from die-hard Indiana Hoosier fans. They told me how much they loved seeing me play football and wished me good luck in my recovery. I read through a couple of the letters, but it was too painful when they discussed football. I wanted nothing to do with it at the time.

Most of my messages were supportive, but there were those who said things like, "What the hell are you going to do with your life now? Everyone knows that once athletes are done with sports, they either go broke or do nothing of significance in the world."

I started to listen to those negative voices. And I started to believe them.

I tried to watch a bit of football on television, hoping that would make the situation a little better, but the exact opposite happened. Seeing other guys playing the game I loved at the highest level broke my spirit even more.

What gives these guys more of a right to be out there than me? I thought. *I should be playing right now.*

I was in such a dark place that I talked to my own parents perhaps only three times during that whole span of two and a half weeks. Rehab didn't start for another week, and all I wanted to do at the moment was stay in bed, feel sorry for myself, and dwell on how terrible my life was.

When you go through a setback, you feel singular. Alone. I knew that numerous NFL players had endured setbacks before, but I could only think about myself and my situation. I pushed away my loved ones, because I didn't want to be perceived as too emotional or vulnerable. Moreover, I was ashamed and fearful of what would happen next. It was more comfortable to drown in self-pity. I was convinced my life was over and that from here on out I would forever be a big loser.

THINGS YOU CAN TACKLE NOW TO OVERCOME DEPRESSION

1. **Talk to friends and family members.** I know now that it would have helped me if I had opened up to friends and family members who were reaching out to me. But I was too wrapped up in myself to realize it. So, next time you're depressed or you're dealing with a large failure, remember

to reach out to those who love you and whom you love. It will help more than you can ever imagine.

2. Be social. Even though I could not do any sports while I was injured, I could have been more social. Being around other people gets you out of your own little world. Go out to dinner with friends, have coffee with a buddy, watch a movie with them, text them, communicate with them via phone, Facebook, or Twitter. The emotional connection will help you understand you're not alone and that all people go through depressing times.

3. Support groups. If the depression is severe, by all means seek out a therapist or join support groups at your local church or community center. Support groups are great, because others can encourage you, give you advice, and share your experiences. Mind you, I didn't do any of these things during my depression, but I know now that it would have helped tremendously.

4. Meditation, walking. Don't forget to check in with a higher power, as I have mentioned before. If you can, go out for walks and get in touch with nature. If you can't walk somewhere, meditate or pray. Just getting in touch with your inner self will help you with this depression.

5. Pets. Having a pet can help anyone in a time of depression. Animals love unconditionally, and they are a great source of comfort when you're hurt and in pain. If you have a dog, take it for a walk. Spend time with it. If you have a cat...well, I have never had a cat, but I've heard they're the boss in most households. However, I also know they can be loving, too. The point is to let yourself love someone, and that someone includes your pets. By opening up your heart to loving others, it will take you outside of yourself and help you tackle the depression.

I believe that when we experience failure, tragedy, or hardship, we all envision the absolute worst outcome. Yes, I was broken and defeated in that moment, but I made it worse because I chose to feel sorry for myself and I refused to take the initiative to improve anything. In times of despair, we must constantly remember to see ourselves beyond our current circumstances. Just like clouds in the sky can temporarily block the sun, the clouds in your life should only be passing through. I struggled desperately to see my life beyond the football field. I wallowed in disappointment and self-pity over things I could not change at the time. It was my own doing. And it was eye-opening and life-changing when I finally realized this.

I'm sure you must feel this way at times. Do you feel that you struggle with the negative experiences in your life? Can you see yourself beyond them? Do you just want to give up and die like I did? Or wallow in self-pity? Do you feel ashamed? Angry?

TACKLE THIS TODAY

When something upsetting happens in your life, do you get angry and believe you're a victim? Or do you take responsibility for your life and create an alternate plan?

The negative experience could be anything—small or big. Maybe you were fired from your job. Maybe you failed at achieving an important goal. Maybe you're battling depression over losing a loved one. Maybe you were rejected by a company or a friend. Maybe something has happened in your personal life that's been difficult for you to come to grips with. Whatever it is, take it from me: There is hope beyond your current state of mind. You just have to think *beyond* yourself.

I remembered Coach Hep and the important life lessons he drilled into my heart when he was alive. I started thinking about football and what the game meant.

TACKLE THIS TODAY

When you look at your life, do you see it as a glass that is half empty or half full? Maybe it is overflowing. The way you view your glass gives you a clue about how you see your life. Why don't you fill up that glass and enjoy the fullness?

I knew that in life, Coach Hep would want me to "keep on moving that ball." To "keep on scoring." He would want me to stop at *nothing* to achieve my goals. But what goals did I have now? They were all gone. I had no Plan B. He had always told me I would be more successful off the field than I ever was on it, but I didn't see how that was possible. My glass felt totally empty, and so did I.

This negative state happens to many people. If there is one thing that completely derails aspiring business owners, athletes, or anyone, for that matter, it is the inability to turn negative experiences into positive ones. It takes a lot of work and practice, and I don't think that it ever becomes an easy thing to do, but once you learn how to stop overanalyzing and beating yourself up over something that didn't go as planned, the better off you will be. It's important to put yourself in a position to grow from that negative experience instead of surrendering to it and remaining stagnant.

I tried to focus on what Coach Hep said: "GBT. Get Better Today." But I couldn't pull myself out of that dark place.

Keep in mind that at that time, I did *nothing* to help myself. I didn't go to church. I didn't pray. I didn't read any motivational or spiritual books. I didn't let any loved ones inside. I ignored my grandparents and my parents and my brother. I didn't talk to anyone. I wouldn't let anyone come near me. I was miserable. Depression kills, and I literally didn't care if someone killed me. I was dead already in my mind.

The Bears offered me the injury settlement to gracefully leave the NFL...and...and...*to do what?* It was up to me, I guess.

I needed to figure out how to get out of that funk and become alive again. But I didn't know how. My longing was too deep. My darkness, too black.

YOUR OWN PERSONAL GAME PLAN TO PUT INTO ACTION

1. Create opportunities. Create your own opportunities instead of waiting for someone to hand them to you. If something happens where you feel broken, but you know there's a dream out there waiting for you, then know this: You can create your own opportunities. It's up to you. If you're passionate about a goal or anything you want to do, create and design the opportunity in the best way you can. For example, if you're interested in a new career but aren't sure what the workplace culture looks like, offer to work as a free intern so you can get some hands-on experience. When I had to move back in with my parents and get a real job, I fretted that my big dream was shattered. Over. Done with. I didn't even think about what I could do to change the situation or create my opportunity. At least, not at first. Finally, I got it and decided to learn all I could about sales and business development in my sales job. The people who wait for the door of opportunity to swing wide open so they can waltz through will likely be waiting a lifetime. Sometimes you have to walk right up to that locked door and break it down.

2. Champions power through. Champions experience rough times like everyone else. But you know what? They simply power through them. I hadn't learned how to be a champion yet when I felt broken and desolate about losing my dream. Since then I've learned that champions develop alternate winning plays that will put them on top. Nothing stops them. They grow stronger through the challenges. If life is easy for you, then you're not going to grow.

It's the difficulties that present the opportunities for growth. One of the biggest mistakes most people make when confronted with failure or a negative experience is they don't look for the positive in the negative. There's value in every experience, no matter if it's a positive or a negative one, and it's up to you to analyze the situation and create an opportunity to turn that negativity into a gift.

Chapter Nine

THE FIGHT FOR RECOVERY

Life always waits for some crisis to occur before revealing itself at its most brilliant.

—*Paulo Coelho*

I would later realize that perhaps one of the most important things in recovery from failure is not self-transformation but self-acceptance. We all have traits and talents that others will appreciate. We simply do not always know what they are. And when we're in the midst of a crisis, it's difficult to believe we're good at anything.

A turning point in my life was about to take place. It would forever change my world.

After being miserable and feeling sorry for myself for more than two weeks, I received a phone call from the office of Stedman Graham, best-selling author and leadership expert. Some of you may know Stedman from his best-selling books, including *Identity: Your Passport to Success*, a *Wall Street Journal* best seller, and others may know of him due to his long-term relationship with Oprah Winfrey. Stedman is also the chairman and CEO of S. Graham and Associates, a Chicago-based management and marketing consulting firm that specializes in corporate and educational markets. One of Stedman's most outstanding qualities is that he is passionate about helping youth and young entrepreneurs.

Publicist A. C. McLean identified himself, and what he said next shocked me. "Look, I know you got hurt during your time with the Bears and that you're not playing football at the moment. Stedman's team wanted me to reach out and invite you to come and speak at his next youth leadership conference."

"Yeah? Did you say Stedman wanted me to come and speak?" I honestly thought he was playing a prank on me.

"Yes, that's right. His nonprofit organization, Athletes Against Drugs, hosts leadership events around the city for the youth. He loves bringing in professional athletes who are positive role models for the community. Can you do it? It's in a couple of weeks," said A.C.

Athletes Against Drugs? I was perplexed, because some people knew about my drug-riddled past, but it wasn't something I talked about regularly, certainly not in a public setting like this.

I had also received a D in public speaking in college, and I was terrified to speak in front of even ten people. After everything that had happened to me, there was no possible way I was going to get up and speak in front of a group of people when I wouldn't even talk to my closest friends and family members.

"Are you serious?" I asked. I still hadn't ruled out that this was a joke.

"Absolutely," A.C. said. "We'd love to have you come and speak if you're not busy."

"I...I'm not sure," I said. *There's no way.*

"Think about it and then get back to me as soon as possible," A.C. said. "We're scheduling all the guest speakers right now and need to know if we can include you. I think you'd be really great, Matt."

"Okay, sure," I said. I didn't believe A.C. for one minute. "Give me a little time to think about it, and I'll call you back."

When I hung up the phone, I immediately thought: *They must be absolutely crazy. This has to be some type of joke or something. Why in the world would they want a former degenerate, who is no longer even playing football, to speak at an upcoming event for Stedman Graham?* I couldn't wrap my head around that. *It's just weird*, I kept telling myself.

I heard a dog bark outside, reminding me that going for a long walk had always made a profound difference for me. A long walk gave me the opportunity to tune out all the outside noise, distractions, and critics and just *think*. It was a form of meditation, and to this day, I have found that it is one of my most useful tools in life.

I wasn't supposed to be walking much with my injury, and it wasn't that easy to move while wearing a walking boot. The doctor had told me that for the first month, I wouldn't be doing any therapy and that I should just relax and try to stay off my foot as much as possible so my ankle could heal. Eventually, I would begin the long and strenuous process of building my range of motion and strength in my ankle. But not yet.

At the time, I honestly didn't care about the doctor or his orders to stay off my foot. I decided to go for a short walk, wearing my big walking boot, to try to make sense of everything that was transpiring.

When I opened the door, the warm air of early autumn hit me in the face. I breathed in deeply, happy to get out of the house. A few yellow leaves were already falling from the trees, scattering in the wind on the sidewalks. I shuffled my feet slowly, then picked up more speed, as I tried to walk as quickly as possible. I was used to days of extreme physicality, and lying around in my bed for more than two weeks had made me sluggish and tired. It felt good to be outside walking, even if my torn ankle still hurt.

For the first time since the injury occurred, I began to see myself more clearly. I was feeling sorry for myself and exaggerating my situation. I was making things much worse than they really were. Did I lose my childhood dream? Yes, I did. Did I have doubts about my future? Absolutely. However, I also realized that kicking myself when I was already down was a surefire way to *stay down*, and I'd never get off that emotional roller coaster if I didn't stop the self-pity.

Six minutes into my walk, it hit me that I had absolutely nothing to lose by embracing the opportunity to speak onstage with Stedman Graham in a couple of weeks. There was no way I could feel worse than I already did, and as much as I hated public speaking, I knew that I had to get moving and take some kind of action instead of sitting in my room all day and night at my parents' house crying about my misfortunes and current sad lot in life.

I pulled my phone out of my pocket and called A.C. "Hey, this is Matt Mayberry."

"Hey, Matt." He paused, waiting for me to continue.

"I'd like to take you up on the offer to speak at Stedman's youth leadership conference if the invitation is still open."

"That's wonderful," A.C. said. "I think you'll be great."

"Thank you for giving me this opportunity," I continued. "I'm very grateful for this."

"We're happy to have you," said A.C. He went on, giving me the details of the event and what I could expect.

When I hung up the phone, I thought, *What in the world am I doing? Can I do this?*

My only public speaking experience had been in college and at random charity events as an athlete. I reminded myself that I got a D in that class and speaking at a charity event "as an athlete" while at Indiana University was no big deal. You could just smile and say, "Go, Hoosiers!" and everyone would clap.

Even though I was scared to death of public speaking, I knew deep down that this was what I needed at the moment. Since the injury, this was the first thing I had decided to embark on outside of lying in my bed and crying myself a river. I had to do it no matter how frightened I was.

That night at dinner after talking to A.C., I sat with my family at the table. My parents and brother had gotten used to me wearing my headphones and completely ignoring them. They had left me alone night after night, being respectful of my need to mourn my loss.

That evening, I looked at them instead of tuning them out and staring at my food. "Um, I got a call today," I told them nonchalantly.

"Who called? Your doctor?" Mom asked.

Dad's eyes immediately brightened. He was glad to hear me say something besides, "I don't want to talk about it."

I explained that I had been invited by Stedman Graham to speak at a youth leadership conference.

Dad put his fork down. A light fell over his face, as if, for the first time in a long time, there were bright days ahead instead of the gloomy ones I had been living in. "That's great."

"What a wonderful opportunity," Mom chimed in.

Even Gary seemed impressed. He knew who Stedman Graham was.

They continued discussing how fantastic it was to speak at a youth leadership conference with Stedman. I didn't want to elaborate much, because honestly I didn't think it was that important. I told them, "It's not a big deal, really."

But that was one of the biggest understatements of my life.

Leading up to the event, I didn't prepare much at all. It would be the first time I had shown my face in public since getting injured, and I was too numb to give it much thought. I assumed it would be just like every other public event I had participated in. I would go onstage, say a couple of words, and five minutes later, I'd shake hands with a bunch of people, smiling and acting like everything was perfectly fine in my life.

When I woke up the morning of my public speaking event, I couldn't take my mind off football. It was still my main passion—my heart and soul—and a game I desperately wanted to play even after I sustained my injury. It hurt so much to watch my college teammates and other friends play in the NFL and have so much fun doing it.

Of course, I was happy for each and every one of them, but I felt like I deserved to be out there, as well. Instead, I was in a freakin' walking boot and getting ready to deliver a short speech at a youth leadership conference.

THINGS YOU CAN TACKLE NOW
TO OVERCOME FEAR

1. Believe in yourself. Whatever it is you're getting ready to do, fully believe that you are more than capable of doing an exceptional job. You must believe in yourself in order to do anything great in this world. When I trained to get my Division I college scholarship, I didn't know how I was going to do it. But when I wholeheartedly believed I could, doors started to open. And when I trained for the NFL, I didn't know if I would ever get the opportunity to play, but I really believed I could do it and eventually did. Don't let doubt and fear stop you from taking that first step. What's the worst thing that can happen? You can fail. But so what? Failure will teach you something about yourself that you didn't know before if you are willing to learn. And as I've been learning throughout my life, failure has been one of my biggest gifts.

2. Beware of your thoughts. It's true. You really are what you think. If you believe you're a failure, you'll remain a failure. But you can succeed if you think, *Sure, I failed, but this failure will help me find something even bigger and better. It's going to make me stronger.* When I sustained my injury in football, I admit I had a hard time believing anything positive was in store for me. So learn from my experience. Be careful of your thoughts and try your best to think positive, uplifting things about yourself. If you keep saying, "I'm afraid of this" or "I'm afraid of that," then your mind will do everything it can to manifest your thoughts. Instead of imagining the *worst-case* scenarios, start thinking of the *best-case* scenarios.

3. Baby steps. Remember, you don't have to climb a mountain in one day. Tiny steps can lead you to a destination just as effectively as giant steps. You may wrestle with your thoughts. You may feel that it's taking too long to reach your goals and that there are too many failures and obstacles along the way. You may be letting fear hold you back. You may give up before you even try. But take it one day, one step at a time. Do not overwhelm yourself by trying to rush or figure out your Plan B quickly if Plan A didn't work.

4. Just do it. Take action even when you're afraid. It's okay to be afraid, but the real magic happens when you move forward despite fear. Power through it and take action anyway. I agreed to speak at Stedman Graham's youth event even though I was afraid I'd fail. I knew I had nothing to lose by trying—by taking action—so I decided to feel the fear and just do it.

5. Action builds self-confidence. When you're willing to take massive action and put yourself out there, no matter how scared you are and no matter how worried you may be, moving forward builds self-confidence. It will open the door to all kinds of new possibilities in your life.

6. Surrender the outcome. When you realize that it doesn't matter if you fail and what really matters is that you've taken action, you can surrender the outcome of the experience. What usually prevents people from trying something new or from taking a risk is that they're afraid they won't succeed. That they'll be ridiculed. No, the outcome isn't guaranteed. But in a way, that's exciting. You never know what will happen, and it just might be the best thing of your life. So surrender those doubts, fears, and negativity and just go for it.

While anticipating the speaking event with Stedman, the doubts and negative thoughts started to eat me up again, and I questioned my ability to stand in front of a crowd and have anything of significance to speak about.

Fear. It was about my fear and doubt—and the negative reinforcement that I continually allowed to take over my thought process.

The whole afternoon leading up to the event, I battled those old inner demons that had been consuming my entire spirit. Demons affect your decision-making ability and everything about your attitude. They prompt you down a dark, depraved path. These demons had consumed me when I was a teenager, and they were surrounding me again. I tried to ignore them, but they were forever needling me, telling me I was no good. A has-been. A washout.

In spite of the demons, I took a shower and put on my best suit. Mom and Dad wished me good luck and I said thanks, but my heart wasn't really in it. Not at the moment.

The beautiful thing about moving forward, despite feeling fear in every muscle in your body and hearing demons call out to you, is that little by little, you start to build up more courage. The movement helps to develop your self-confidence, which, at this point in my life, was absolutely crucial.

TACKLE THIS TODAY

Movement helps to build courage. Just get up and do it. Whatever it is that you've been afraid to do, now is the time to do it. The movement adds to the creation of our personal journey, and the only way we're going to achieve our dreams and goals is to start moving.

After flirting with fear and doubt and trying to convince myself that I wasn't worthy enough to step onstage with a best-selling author and a world-renowned figure like Stedman Graham, I now know that I made one of the best decisions of my life.

When I arrived at the youth leadership conference, A.C. immediately welcomed me and shook my hand. "I know you're going to do a great job." He gave me the itinerary and told me where to sit until it was time for my presentation.

I was to speak right before Stedman. With hands sweating and pulse racing, I waited. Finally, Art Norman, the emcee and legendary news anchor for NBC Chicago, introduced me.

I walked onstage and ended up giving a speech about having a strong work ethic and persevering until you achieve your goals. As I left the stage, everyone stood and started clapping. I was shocked.

Euphoria swept over me—a kind of lightness in my heart that I hadn't felt in a long, long time—and it was right then and there that I discovered my true purpose and life's calling.

I remembered what Coach Hep had said: "Football is *what* you do; it's not *who* you are."

For the first time, I understood and I believed him.

All this time, I had been beating myself up and even contemplating death just because I lost what I'd *thought* was my biggest dream in the world. Little did I know that dream was a stepping-stone—a building block—to discover my *real* dream and true life's mission. All along I believed it was sports. My major in college had been Recreational Sports Management, and I had always assumed my career would revolve around sports.

That's the funny thing about life, though. Right when you think you have everything figured out or know what your major life dream is, in the blink of an eye that dream can break down and unravel. It's in those moments of darkness where real greatness and opportunity exist. That's why so many people go to their graves with their dreams and talents lying dormant inside them. They never took the chance to explore them. They let fear, circumstances, doubt, or lack of self-confidence stop them from chasing their dreams. They didn't trust that maybe there was something better waiting for them.

Even though I didn't want to speak at Stedman's event that night, something inside me had told me to do it. And I'm so glad I listened.

We all need to learn how to listen to our inner guidance, especially in moments of despair. You are smarter and stronger than you think you are. If there is one thing I can promise you, it would be this: You have the power and ability to change your circumstances and start the process of building a bigger future for yourself right at this exact moment. If I can do it, then you are capable of just as much, if not more!

I then watched Stedman speak and was moved by his passion for helping the youth, athletes, and young entrepreneurs. He was extremely polished and professional. Stedman talked about how important it was to create your own identity and that if you didn't, the world would do it for you. I admired him. He was making a tremendous difference in the world. By comparison, when I looked at myself, I saw nothing of value.

Even though I was full of self-doubt, I was still happy from my quick experience onstage.

When the evening started to wind down, I went up to Stedman and shook his hand. "I just want to tell you how much I appreciate you inviting me and having me onstage to speak with you."

"My pleasure, Matt," he said warmly. "You did a great job."

"Thank you," I said. I paused, shuffled my feet, and put my hands into my pockets. I didn't intend to say more, but I blurted out, "You know, I can't believe how amazing it felt. I would love to do this more often."

Stedman looked straight into my eyes. "It's an extremely rewarding career. You have something special. You should do it."

"What do you mean? As a career?" I had a hard time believing it. I knew there were people who did it, of course, but surely not people like me! I mean, this was *fun*.

"Yes, as a career," Stedman said. "Not only can you make a living doing it, but the reward and deep sense of satisfaction knowing that you're really helping others is one of the best feelings in the world."

I was in complete shock. I had no idea that someone like

me could make a living speaking and positively impacting people's lives. I saw the way Stedman was living his life and the impact he was making in the world, and I was completely blown away that he thought I could do it, too. I now wanted to feel that *exact same feeling* in my own life. I wanted that same fulfillment.

And then it dawned on me: Football wasn't my true purpose in life. It was just something I did. Coach Hep had told me that. But now *I got it*. Football was great, and in many ways it had saved my life. It gave me a college degree from a top university, life-changing opportunities, and confidence and pride, but it had been my stepping-stone, my bridge to a better life. It didn't completely satisfy my heart and soul and bring me lasting happiness every morning when I woke up to begin my day. It didn't fulfill me like I knew speaking could.

Sure, before my injury, I could make people smile and enjoy their weekends as they watched me play football, but that was miniscule in comparison to what Stedman was doing. Through his writing and speaking, he was changing lives and impacting people's worlds and happiness. I was fascinated by this revelation.

Art Norman, who is now a great friend of mine, came up to me. "You are a phenomenal speaker. You're going to be a star one day."

A star? What is he talking about? I looked at him like he was kind of crazy, because in my eyes I hadn't done anything special. I hadn't even prepared! I simply told the audience about the things it took to become great and how I was able to overcome adversity. I didn't mention drugs or my dark past, because I didn't have the courage to open up about it yet. It was as if divine intervention was calling to me. This event was to benefit the Athletes Against Drugs foundation, and I was an athlete who once was addicted to drugs that almost took my life, but no one here even knew that. It was like the world was telling me something. Beckoning me to my true calling. Quietly awakening my purpose.

TACKLE THIS TODAY

Never underestimate the value of a hard work ethic. It will help you reach your goals and become the person you were always meant to be.

At the end of the evening, people ran up to me and asked if they could take a selfie with me. They told me how much they loved and appreciated the speech I had just given. I couldn't believe it. I was moved.

TACKLE THIS TODAY

Babies are necessary to grown-ups. A new baby is like the beginning of all things—wonder, hope, a dream of possibilities.

—Eda J. LeShan

Are you like a baby? Are you the beginning of all things? I was after speaking with Stedman Graham. I was the new beginning of myself and a dream of possibilities. What are your dreams of possibilities?

This was another magical moment, just like the time I had an epiphany when I was sixteen and finally looked at myself in the mirror.

When I left Stedman's youth leadership event that night, the air had turned cooler and the wind had picked up. Stars flooded the sky with sparkles, and crickets chirped. But I don't remember much else. I was too overwhelmed.

When I got to my car and settled into my seat, I put the key into the ignition. But before turning it, I stopped. I completely broke down and cried, thanking God for what had just happened. In this special moment I didn't care about football, my injury, or even where my future was headed. That was how I knew right then and there that this was my purpose and passion and what God had put me on earth to do. Something had dramatically changed within me.

I didn't know how I was going to make it happen, but I knew I had a story to tell that the world desperately needed to hear. They needed to hear that they—like me—have *more* inside them. They needed to hear that they absolutely can live their best lives regardless of how many times they've failed or how unlucky they may think they are. I had to tell everyone!

When failure knocks you down, it can be the best thing that ever happened to you. It can be the first day of a new life. It can be a new beginning, not an end. And instead of waiting for the right opportunity to come along, you can work with the opportunity in front of you no matter what it is. If you are determined, you can make the best of it and pull out every bit of goodness you can from it.

I recognized that uniting with positive, like-minded people was important. Stedman Graham was one of those. He had achieved his dreams and was continuing to build new ones. I believe success is contagious. And if you connect with successful, positive people, it will bring out the best in you. Since that night, I have surrounded myself with the best and brightest writers, executives, speakers, and best-selling authors like Matthew Kelly, Jon Gordon, and numerous others. They have mentored me and guided me. They make me better every single day. And that brings me to Coach Hep and his motto: GBT. Uniting with positive, like-minded people is helping me get better today...and tomorrow.

INCREASING ACTION WHEN FEAR AND NEGATIVITY AFFECT YOUR LIFE

Later on, the whole experience with Stedman Graham reminded me of how I had been letting fear and negativity control my life. I knew that it happened to everyone, especially salespeople. Throughout the years I have had the great privilege to train and work with some of the most amazing sales organizations in the world, and to me, sales is one of the best examples of the importance of increasing action when adversity strikes.

As a salesperson, you are going to be told no more than yes. For most people, this is tough to deal with. Let's face it—nobody likes rejection. The average salesperson hates how they feel when they are told no, so they might end up making fewer calls, visiting fewer prospects, and doing just enough to keep their jobs.

Unfortunately, that doesn't apply only to salespeople.

People from all walks of life seemingly have adopted that philosophy for when the going gets tough. Just do enough to get by. It will be okay. *Um...no, it's not okay.*

On the other side of the spectrum, you have the salespeople who continue to increase their income regardless of how bad the economy is. The value they bring to both the marketplace and their companies is impressive. Everyone asks them how they do it, looking for some magical answer or secret. In reality, these overachievers aren't doing anything magical; they constantly take massive action by studying the market and trying new things to develop and achieve business goals, even when the going gets tough.

The best salespeople understand that if they made thirty calls the previous day and received thirty rejections, then they have to make sixty calls the following day to possibly get one yes.

TACKLE THIS TODAY

Are you doing just enough to get by? Or are you increasing your action and forever looking for new ways to grow and excel? Are you doing the things that can take you to the next level in your job, career, or personal life?

Increasing your action when adversity strikes can be a complete game changer. It will bring far more results than taking the easy way out. When you increase action, you increase the chance of opportunities coming your way.

It's nearly impossible to defeat the person who is willing to get back up and keep fighting. Regardless of how devastating your failures have been or how often you've found yourself in the gutter, if you never get complacent and *settle* for just getting by, then failure and hard times won't be able to bury you in darkness. I've been there, and I know what it feels like. Mediocrity can paralyze you and keep you from tapping into your inner greatness.

Some of the world's greatest achievers weren't necessarily more talented; they just never gave up. Get moving. Take action. The whole moral behind increasing your action is to take complete charge of what's to come.

Most of the time when people experience a major failure, they just sit back and wait for life to happen. That's what I had been doing when I was injured. It's easy to fall into a slump when something takes away your dream. But it was an invaluable learning experience.

Over time you will learn that waiting for life to happen serves no purpose. I didn't know that speaking at the leadership event would introduce me to my purpose or help me view failure in a different light, but it did. It was all because I decided to get out of bed, stop feeling sorry for myself, and begin moving, even though I was afraid and had no confidence whatsoever.

When failure knocks you down, taking massive action gives you self-confidence. Failure in itself becomes a graveyard for so many. The fear of failure grows so strong that any chance of getting started is zero, and the likelihood of pursuing a dream or passion is slim to none.

Failure combined with *inaction* is extremely deadly. One

of the best things you can do for yourself right now is to resolve that you won't wait for things to be perfect, because things will never be perfect. Just get moving!

So, in the end, the fight for recovery wasn't about working to heal my ankle. Rather, it was to find meaning in my life and rebuild the life I had.

Mark Twain supposedly said, "The two most important days of your life are the day you are born and the day you find out why."

That night after speaking onstage, I discovered the *why* behind why I was born. And it was brilliant! My life would never be the same again.

YOUR OWN PERSONAL GAME PLAN
TO PUT INTO ACTION

1. Listen to the music. Please do not die with your music still inside you. This means that you may have to open yourself to unknown possibilities that present themselves to you out of nowhere. I don't know what would have happened if I had not gone to speak at Stedman Graham's youth leadership event that night. Would I have eventually been awakened to my life's passion? Surely, I would have. But it chills me when I think I might have gone to my deathbed with that music still inside me. Thank goodness I decided to step out of my comfort zone and speak that night alongside Stedman. Make it a goal of yours to do something that scares you daily. Be a risk taker. Have some fun with it, and enlist a group of friends to participate in this game with you. Pick one thing every day. It doesn't matter how big or small it is—whether it's learning something new or experimenting with a different style or look—but make sure you do it.

2. Redirections. Failures and setbacks can be blessings in disguise. And when it comes time to redirect your life or stay stagnant where you are, you must open yourself to the possibility and the redirection. If you don't, the blessing will pass you by. I've met numerous people who were closed off about what they wanted to do with their lives. They simply weren't open to other possibilities. One man told me he wanted a job in a particular part of the city on an exact street. I said, "Aren't you worried that you're limiting yourself by being so narrow-minded and specific?" He looked at me like I was crazy and said, "That is where I want to be, and I won't be happy if I'm not there." I doubt he found a job. He was too closed-minded. Think of all the college students across the country who spend a significant amount of money on an education and then end up doing something totally different the minute they graduate. Teachers often start their own businesses, too. Many people redirect their lives either out of necessity or passion. When we are open to other possibilities and redirections, we are more apt to achieve our goals.

Chapter Ten

THE AWAKENING

If you can imagine it, you can achieve it. If you can dream it, you can become it.

—*William Arthur Ward*

Little by little, the impenetrable crust had cracked open in my sorry old soul, and the light poured through in waves of gold, eclipsing the darkness that had been my constant companion for the past couple of months.

After speaking with Stedman and sitting in my car with tears streaming down my face that evening, it dawned on me for the first time in my life that everything that happens to us is for a reason. Every adversity, every failure, every heartbreak truly does have an equal or greater seed of opportunity planted within it. There I was, thinking for the longest time that luck was not on my side. That I was a loser. There was high school and the drug addiction, the failure to get drafted in the NFL, then the brief time I played for the Chicago Bears—a childhood dream of mine—and bam! Over and out with one injury. Darkness closed off all the light in my little world.

I truthfully thought that my life sucked. That I had no luck and that God didn't want me to win at anything. I looked at every situation and failure in my life without ever analyzing myself and uncovering what was beneath the skin of Matt Mayberry.

I easily could have continued to stay and wallow in my bed after the ankle injury and cry myself to sleep every single night without ever doing anything to change my situation. Thank God I didn't.

TACKLE THIS TODAY

There's only one corner of the universe you can be certain of improving, and that's your own self.

—*Aldous Huxley*

What I have learned about life throughout my journey so far is that most people *say* they want their circumstances to change. They go on to talk about how much they hate where they are, but then they never do anything about it. You can't just hope for a better future or life without doing anything about it.

I didn't know that when I received the invitation to speak alongside Stedman Graham that it would point me to an entirely new career and change the rest of my life forever. In the face of adversity or some type of hardship, the power of moving forward can be life-changing.

After the speaking event, I was on cloud nine. I could go

on and on about how amazing I felt. There was something magical—even spiritual—about the entire experience. It was one of those golden moments when the stars seem to be in perfect alignment with your thoughts. When the moon glows brighter and even the air seems sweeter and clearer. And you know without a shadow of a doubt that you're on to something *big*. That was exactly how I felt as I sat there in my car sobbing.

I had been awakened. That's the only way I can describe it.

When I finally turned the ignition, stepped on the gas pedal, and drove home that night, I felt like a brand-new person. I had been *awakened* to a potential in me that I didn't even know existed before. Football didn't cross my mind, and even more shockingly, I didn't think for a split second about my injury or how terrible I previously thought my life was. It was gone! Just like that.

I walked in the door to my parents' house, smiling and energetic. Not more than three hours ago, I had left the house in the dumps and mad at the world.

Mom stood there with her mouth open and gaped at me. Obviously, she couldn't believe her eyes. "Is everything okay?"

I grinned.

"Are you high?" There was worry in her face.

I laughed and flashed her a bigger smile. "Yes, yes, I'm *high*, but this is a different kind of high. I swear, I'm not on drugs."

"But...but—," she began.

"Mom, for the first time in my life, I know what it feels like to be high on life. It sounds like a cliché, but it's true."

She had a blank look on her face. She was speechless.

I explained the whole event with speaking onstage along-side Stedman, our conversation, and how I had experienced an epiphany about what to do with my life.

"That's wonderful," Mom said. "I'm just so happy you didn't go back to the drugs."

I don't think she really understood what I was talking about. She thought I had a good time speaking, and it had brought me out of my depression. And that made her happy. To be honest, she was just happy that I hadn't gotten back into drugs.

Dad had the same reaction as Mom when he came down-stairs. He smiled and told me it was great that I had a good time. He and Mom exchanged a few looks, though. They were still concerned about my "odd" behavior.

In the following weeks, my parents were happy for me, of course, but I knew for a fact that they didn't fully under-stand what I meant when I told them I had discovered my true purpose. But they didn't argue with me because they saw how excited I was with this new goal and direction. They didn't want to interfere with my peace of mind given the wreck I had been.

It was hard to explain to anybody. But it was real—*this golden, magical feeling that I had been awakened to a new life*. I knew public speaking was exactly what I wanted to do the minute after Stedman told me that I could turn it into a career.

I admit that running out of the tunnel at Indiana Uni-versity onto the football field with eighty thousand to a hundred thousand screaming fans had been an exhilarating experience. But the high I got from speaking in front of a group of people who responded positively to what I said was different. It came from a place deeper within my spirit. *My heart and soul.* It had awakened an inner strength and joy that I never knew I possessed.

How in the world would I become a public speaker? I didn't know how it was going to happen, but I started to read every motivational and inspirational book I could find. I searched the Internet for "how to become a better speaker."

I took Coach Hep's "Get Better Today" motto to heart. I could do this with public speaking the same way I had done it with sports.

I have always loved working hard. During my entire life up to this point, I never shied away from putting in the long hours needed to master a craft and striving to become the best I could possibly be. This work ethic had been drilled into me since I was little. Grampa Dee and Dad worked this way and taught me to do the same. Coach Hep and other coaches taught me to do this, as well.

At the time, I lacked the necessary resources and experience to make a living at public speaking. It would be an uphill battle for me, but I was determined to succeed. I was persistent. A hard worker. A go-getter. I had never felt so passionate about anything else before. I intended to turn this dream into a reality and make it a genuinely successful career.

So I began doing everything possible to fulfill this passion of mine. I searched the Internet and studied books night and day. I continually stood in front of the mirror and rehearsed

giving speeches. I made my parents, little brother, and grandparents gather in the living room and sit there and pretend
they were in the audience while I gave talks. And I practiced,
practiced, practiced.

TACKLE THIS TODAY

If there's anything you want to do, tackle it with every
ounce of energy you have. Research it, read books
about it, find mentors who will help guide you, and
then practice, practice, practice.

And then it happened.

I couldn't believe it.

It was a miracle.

It came completely out of nowhere. I received a phone
call from a local community organization that had heard
about me being a "pretty good speaker." Keep in mind that I
thought I was crap. That D in public speaking I had received
in college was foremost on my mind. But I figured I was getting the invitation because I was local, and it wouldn't cost
them much money.

The truth is, it didn't matter what they paid me. I would
have done it for free. I can't remember exactly, but I think
they paid me five hundred dollars.

I was ecstatic, and I couldn't believe what was going on.
It was like God had reached out and called me on the phone.

I gladly accepted their offer to speak. All of this came

from my *awakening* and was literally the beginning of a new life for me. I was starting to believe in *me* again.

THINGS YOU CAN TACKLE NOW TO AWAKEN TO A NEW DREAM

1. Identify your dream. Many people don't know what they should be doing with their lives. In fact, most probably don't. But people know when they're unhappy with the life they have. Perhaps you realize there is something else you should be doing with your life, but you're not sure what it is. You want to awaken to a new dream, but what is it? To find out, first make a list of things you love to do. Write down a goal or a dream that excites you, allows you to grow, and fulfills you.

2. Think like a child. It's helpful to remember yourself as a child and to become childlike again. What did you love to do? Did you enjoy pretending to be an athlete, a spouse, a teacher, an entertainer of some sort? Oftentimes, our childhood loves are clues to what we should be doing with our lives. I pretended to be Walter Payton all the time, running around and throwing footballs. I don't remember wanting to be a public speaker, but I wasn't aware of public speaking as a career. I liked the performance aspect of being an athlete, and that's a clue in itself. Public speaking is performing, and it is something that's natural and comfortable for me. In the same way, there's something for you that's perfect.

3. Dream. Let yourself dream and fantasize about being in that new career or achieving that new goal. Dreaming about it will help you achieve it. Visualize yourself doing whatever it is you want to do. Perhaps we haven't thought about our dreams for a long, long time, but all of them are still within us. If you're unhappy with what you're doing now, at some point, you have dreamed of a different life. Maybe you've forgotten those dreams or you've become too bogged down by the daily grind to consider them again. Don't forget that it's never, ever too late.

4. Brainstorm. Start brainstorming about all the careers out there. Search the Internet and read about companies, jobs, and careers that appeal to you. Do any of them make you smile and go, "Aha! Boy, I would love that!" If so, that might be a clue for you.

5. Choose. Simply identify two or three careers that you'd love. Then prioritize them. What's the number one thing you'd love to do? Next, write down the steps you need to achieve that number one dream. Research others who have succeeded in that career and find out how they did it. If you can, create a plan that follows in their footsteps. In other words, take action—any kind of action at all—and get started on awakening to that new dream and achieving it.

After that event for the local sales organization, word of mouth spread fast, and more organizations, associations, and companies started inviting me to speak to their employees. I had never once planned on speaking to a bunch of businesses or even tapping into the corporate marketplace, but my athleticism, work ethic, sense of teamwork, and discipline were topics that resonated with most companies. They all wanted me to come in and bring my passion to help motivate their employees.

During the following weeks after the event with Stedman and while I was being invited to speak at organizations, I went to physical rehab to work on my ankle. Generally, I'd go in the morning for two or three hours, then research ways to get more speaking engagements. I developed more stories that I could use to share with audiences and really make a difference in their lives.

For eight months while I was injured, I would rehab my ankle and work on my dreams to be a public speaker. I ended up speaking over twenty-five times during the span of my injury rehabilitation and while I wasn't playing football. Although it felt amazing to speak all around the city and be treated like I was a champion again, I was barely bringing in enough money to make a living so I could move out into my own place.

I still missed playing football, of course, but more than playing the actual sport, I missed my teammates and the togetherness that the sport demands. There is a culture in football and in all sports, and I suddenly was not part of that culture. I truly loved that aspect of the game, and it was one of the few things that I still missed after I discovered my true purpose and passion.

Everyone in my life at the time, even my closest friends and family members, believed I would give football another try once I was completely healed and cleared to play again.

Grampa Dee talked about it. "Matt, you'll be up and on

the field in no time. This is just a little blip in your career. It's not a big deal, you know."

Dad talked about it, too. "It won't be long before you're out there. You'll be stronger than ever."

But deep down, I had a different plan. I didn't tell anyone about it at the time, but I was reprogramming my life. I was going through a reboot, a rejuvenation, an awakening. Like a newborn baby, I was being born again.

My dreams and goals now included speaking and traveling the world and writing my stories, so I could impact thousands and thousands of people's lives no matter what their ages were. I wanted to impact the young and old alike. This was what I intended to do every day for the rest of my life.

Getting the chance to speak with Stedman and the numerous organizations afterward had reignited the fire in me. And it burned with the brightness of a million suns.

I knew that my friends and family still wanted to see me on the football field again. Matt, the football player, was all they really knew, and they loved that Matt, so I didn't argue with them. I simply decided to keep everything to myself. Once I started the official process of building a business on my own, I would tell them.

I had no prior knowledge of business, no MBA, and no one to guide me and show me the right and wrong way to do things. But I knew I would find the way.

The time came for me to get back to playing football, and everyone around me had a difficult time containing their excitement.

TACKLE THIS TODAY

To be what we are, and to become what we are capable of becoming, is the only end of life.

—*Robert Louis Stevenson*

What do you believe you are capable of becoming? Are you ready to start?

I knew my ankle was nowhere near ready, considering the fact that I was still having a difficult time cutting on the field and running full speed. However, when the doctors tested my ankle, they said it was healing properly and I would be ready in a week or so to start training 100 percent and playing football again.

Everyone was excited for me, and the texts and phone calls came in left and right.

My agent got word of the results and was ecstatic. "I'm very optimistic that a team will want you now—at least on their practice squad—but you'll have to show them that your ankle is fully healed and that you can run and perform just like you were doing before you got injured."

"Uh-huh," I said. "I figured they would want to see the X-rays." I didn't say much else to my agent at the time.

He called me a couple days later, all fired up and excited about my future. "There are three NFL teams who want to see you work out to see how healthy you are. I told them you were doing fantastic."

As my agent rambled on, I thought about it long and hard

for ten minutes, and then quietly said, "Thanks for all your help, but I'm not going to play football anymore."

"What do you mean that you will no longer be playing football? Are you crazy? Rookie free agents hardly ever get a second chance in the NFL, and this is a great opportunity for you to prove that you belong."

He was an agent who was phenomenal at his job, and I understood his initial frustration.

When I spoke again, my voice was quiet. "My college coach—Coach Hep—always told me that football was *what* I did and not *who* I am, and now I clearly understand what he was telling me so long ago."

"What do you mean?" I could hear the disappointment in his voice.

"During my time off, I had a wonderful opportunity to do some soul-searching, which ultimately led me to my life's work and purpose." I paused for a moment, thinking my agent would question me or yell about how crazy I was, but he didn't say a word.

"Football never excited me so much that I could not sleep at night," I continued. "Football never had me obsessed all day and all night about what my next move was going to be. Yes, football has brought happiness into my life—you know that—and I have loved every minute of it. But speaking onstage and impacting others brings an everlasting joy and happiness to my soul and spirit that I cannot fully describe. I'm sorry, but I will no longer be playing football, so you can tell all of them that I appreciate the opportunity very much, but no thanks."

"Are you 100 percent sure that this is what you want to do?" He sounded stunned.

"I am absolutely sure," I said.

"Matt, I'm sorry to see you go, but I wish you the best of luck. I'll be here for you if you ever change your mind or need me."

"Thanks. I appreciate that," I told him.

The minute we hung up I knew I had made the right decision. It was so magical that it felt like I wasn't even the one making this decision. It felt like I was guided, and whether that guidance came from Coach Hep, God, or a guardian angel, I am forever thankful.

My family and friends couldn't believe it when I told them that I planned to start speaking and writing full-time. Everyone laughed at me and said that I was out of my mind, kind of like my agent did, although they were more blunt about it.

I got lectured about how I made the wrong decision and there was no way I could write or speak full-time and actually make money from it.

Their assumptions were partially correct, because during the few months that I was speaking while I was injured and in rehabilitation, I wasn't making nearly enough to move into my own place and survive on my own. Out of the twenty-plus public speaking events, I earned five hundred dollars here and there, and once I got paid two thousand dollars, which was huge for me at the time. But I didn't care about the money; I cared about how I impacted others' lives and the euphoria I felt knowing I had made a real difference in someone's life and world.

TACKLE THIS TODAY

When you have a dream, you cannot let the naysayers sway you from going after it. There will always be the ones who tell you that you are an idiot for thinking you can do something out of the ordinary. Prove them wrong.

Of course I had to earn money to survive, as money is the oxygen for any business and life. Without it, there is no business, no life. But I told myself over and over again that I would find a way to make it work. I believed in my dream, and I knew that the money would follow.

One of the pioneering books that professed these very ideas and philosophies was *Do What You Love, the Money Will Follow: Discovering Your Right Livelihood* by Marsha Sinetar. Published by Dell in 1989, this book went on to be an international best seller and was the forerunner of other more modern and similar books, including *Intentional Living: Choosing a Life That Matters* by best-selling author John C. Maxwell.

Some things never really go out of style, and *Do What You Love, the Money Will Follow* proves it. In her book, Sinetar explores how people do what they do and why they *do not do* what they love because they are so focused on the money and simply earning a living. Right in the beginning, Sinetar states that the money may not materialize immediately and maybe not at all. For those of us who were not born with a strong character and hard work ethic, it takes real courage to act on what we value. Those who are truly successful achieve not only because they love what they do and are good at it, but because they have the courage to act on their convictions. In her book she illustrates how to tune in to your inner world and unique talents, how to evaluate and build your self-esteem, how to overcome resistance, how to take risks, and how to get rid of the *I should*s.

When my ankle was healed, I worked out at the gym in the morning before focusing on my business. Then I worked out after I was finished with business for the day. Working out has always been a major outlet for me and still is. It's when I clear my mind and deal with the stresses of my day.

Doubt circled me from every angle, and negativity bombarded me like torpedoes hurling from the sky. At times it was difficult to stay positive with so many people telling me I would fail. But I was like a racehorse, champing at the bit, rarin' to go, and ready to be crowned champion at the Kentucky Derby. I was prepared to annihilate the negativity and prove everyone wrong who had doubted me. I was determined to show them that I could become more successful *outside* of football than I ever was *in* football.

But even young, talented stallions aren't always ready to compete in the Kentucky Derby. I've heard trainers talk about two-year-old racehorses that breeze a furlong or two at a fast pace, but they know only raw running and understand very little of actual racing. Perhaps I was like the young stallion that was talented and eager to go. I just knew very little about the business.

Two weeks flew by, and no one called and invited me to speak at their company. Four weeks went by, and still no one called. I fidgeted. I worked out in the gym. I kept to myself and didn't go out with friends. I was focused, but now I was getting nervous.

Two and a half months passed, and still there were no calls. After my full recovery, I had not made a single dime from my new writing and speaking business. I couldn't believe it. I was dumbfounded.

TACKLE THIS TODAY

Whatever you think you can do, or believe you can do, begin it, because action has magic, grace and power in it.

—attributed to Johann Wolfgang von Goethe

The test comes when you know you have a dream and you are going to do all you can to achieve it. But what happens when it fails? What happens when it seems as if everything is stacked against you and you are tempted to go back to your old ways? What do you do?

I felt myself spiraling into déjà vu moments of unworthiness and doubt. In tiny spaces, I felt the old calling of drugs. I felt myself rewinding to moments of darkness and anger. Dangerous places. On-the-edge places.

I thought I was once and for all finished with those hardships that knocked me down and closed off the light. I wasn't sure how much more I could take after the roller-coaster ride of emotions that I had been on for the past ten years.

Of course, realistically, I knew nothing about building

a business. I was young and naïve. A young stallion full of energy and buckaroo wildness. Full of talent and promise. But I didn't have a clue about how to build my business. And I didn't have a penny to my name.

As I attempted to construct my speaking and writing career, I incorporated personal training into my advertisements and promotions on my website. But when I included fitness training along with speaking, I think it confused a lot of people. They didn't know exactly what I did. Was I a personal trainer? A maximum performance strategist? Or was I a public speaker?

I read entrepreneurship books, acquired new skills, and invested in positive relationships. I surrounded myself with people I admired and could learn from.

TACKLE THIS TODAY

Be realistic about what you need to do today to achieve those dreams. It is okay to declare that you need help. A baby needs help when he's learning how to walk and navigate the world. In the same way, when you begin a new venture that has not been part of your education or world, you will need to get new education from mentors, schools, books, leaders, and others who can help you.

It wasn't until I started to thoroughly study business and learn from mentors that I realized I had to be extremely clear about who I was, what I did, and what I could offer people and companies. Combining the fitness training and public speaking was one of the reasons I failed at first. I trained clients in fitness and then tried to go out into the business world and talk about performance and success. Sometimes it worked, but as a promotional and advertising message, it failed.

Don't get me wrong. I still talk about the importance of health and fitness with all my corporate clients and audiences, because that's an integral part of a strong mind and physiology. Being healthy and fit helps people endure, persevere, and succeed.

When my business was failing, I tried cold-calling people, but no one would accept me as a public speaker at their company events. What was I doing wrong?

I had spoken twenty-plus times while I was injured and hobbling around in a walking boot. How did that happen? And now when I was healed and ready and raring to go into public speaking full-time, no one wanted me. It didn't make sense to me. I had expected things to happen too quickly. But in reality, building a successful business takes time and forethought.

I had received a settlement from the Bears when I was let go. It was nominal and absolutely fair for my circumstances. But that meant I had no money to support myself while I was building my business. So I was broke and living at home with my parents.

Here we go again, I thought. I was lost and confused, unsure of what to do next. I felt defeated.

Grampa Dee suggested I get a job. *A real job.* Something that would pay the bills.

What in the world could I do?
I was clueless.

YOUR OWN PERSONAL GAME PLAN
TO PUT INTO ACTION

1. Find out your why. This means that if you identify a dream or a goal you want to pursue, ask yourself why. Is it because it will put the music in your heart? Will it fulfill the creative stirring that's welling up inside you? Or do you want this goal because it will make you rich? I remember hearing college guys talk about wanting to become physicians. When I asked why, a couple of them said, "Because I'll get rich." I couldn't help but think that was the wrong answer. I would never want to go to a physician who was in it for the money. I believe that to be truly fulfilled and happy, you must follow your bliss. You must embrace a purpose-driven life and serve mankind in some way. For me, it was simple. I wanted to change people's lives through my speaking and writing. I wanted to share everything I had learned with everyone else. And, yes, friends and family were shocked when they learned that I didn't want to play professional football anymore. But my mind was made up. I wanted to live my purpose. That's what tugged at my heart. I strongly believe that each and every one of us was put here to fulfill a specific purpose. When you find out what that purpose is, I can promise you that your life will never be the same again. Mark Twain reportedly said, "The two most important days of your life are the day you are born and the day you find out why." If you haven't yet found out what your why is or discovered your true purpose, answer the following questions. They may help steer you in the right direction.

- *What tugs at your heart and keeps you up with excitement at night?* I loved football, but it never tugged at my heart and kept me up with so much excitement at night that I couldn't sleep. On the other hand, speaking and impacting the lives of others absolutely did and still does to this day.

- *What makes you cry?* Best-selling author John C. Maxwell says, "Finding our purpose requires us to seek to discover two things: our passion, and our giftedness. What is the deep desire set in your heart, the thing that sets your soul on fire? What makes you cry? What do you get most excited about? And what are you good at? No one else in the world has exactly the same gifts, talents, background, or future that you do."* When you identify what makes you cry, and what sets your soul on fire, and you tap into those, you begin to understand your why.

- *What would you do if your days were numbered?* If you went to the doctor for a routine checkup and received unexpected news that you were terminally ill and had a very short time left to live, what would you do? I asked myself this before I told my agent that I would no longer be playing football. I thought of many things I wanted to do, but football wasn't one of them. Speaking and making a difference in the lives of others was at the forefront of everything I wanted to do.

---

* John C. Maxwell, "What I Believe About Success," JohnMaxwell.com, March 5, 2014; johnmaxwell.com/blog/what-I-believe-about-success.

Chapter Eleven

MAKING MY LIFE WHOLE AGAIN: "HOUR OF GREATNESS"

Fear stifles our thinking and actions. It creates indecisiveness that results in stagnation. I have known talented people who procrastinate indefinitely rather than risk failure. Lost opportunities cause erosion of confidence, and the downward spiral begins.

—*Charles Stanley*

I believed I was a survivor of numerous failures and that the wounds were healed, but I discovered there were still deep gashes in my soul filled with disillusionment, disappointment, and doubt—fragile things that ached longingly for something more. The bright, burning fire in me had gone out, and the smoke had exhausted itself.

Then I began to wonder if my dreams were too big and too good to be true. If all the miracles that I thought had taken place were just an illusion, a trickery of the worst kind.

I felt like a failure all over again. *I mean, how can this be happening once more?* However, something was different this time. *I still had hope!* I clung to that hope like a lifeline. I knew if I let go of it, I'd find myself back in that bleak, dangerous place.

What helped me remain hopeful and believe that everything would eventually work out for the best was being able to examine everything that I had already overcome. I had been in much darker places before, and I recognized that failing at a speaking career was a tiny thing compared to some of those other challenges.

Remembering the adversities I had already overcome gave me the hope and reassurance I desperately needed after that current setback in the public speaking world. I knew that if I could just work through this, the setback would give me tremendous perspective.

Sometimes the pain we experience during a hardship or a failure is so excruciating that we want to forget it and never think about it again. But on the other side of the spectrum, I believe it is important to remember how strong we really are and that we can get through another failure, another hardship, another trial in life. We can all do it, and we'll be the stronger for it.

When Grampa Dee suggested I get a job, I resisted at first. I had found my true passion and I knew that was what I wanted to do. But reality set in. I was an adult, and I couldn't depend on my parents to support me. I had to take responsibility for my life. Also, I realized that I was out of my mind to assume that I would be able to just jump right into running a successful public speaking business after speaking only a few times.

I felt defeated, miserable, and aggravated that I had to put my dreams on hold and get a job I wasn't passionate about. I talked often about how I never wanted to be one of those people who went to work every day at a job they absolutely hated.

Grampa Dee told me, "Look, a job could actually help you get to where you want to go. You could look at it as a way to support you while you're building that professional speaking career."

What he said made sense. Grampa Dee and the rest of my family simply wanted me to be happy, but I knew that many of them secretly believed I could not earn a living as a public speaker and writer. I knew many people doubted me.

I wanted to prove to everyone that I would become more successful outside of football than I ever was while playing football. I honestly repeated what Coach Hep had told me every single day. That football was *what* I did and not *who* I was. I knew I was so much more, and I was determined to become the absolute best that I could be.

Getting a regular job would not only bring financial stability, but it would also increase my skill set in certain areas. I wanted to develop in business, sales, marketing, and grow my professional network. The corporate world would be a great place to do this, and I could carry these skills over into my own business development. I had my degree in Recreational Sports Management from Indiana University. I didn't have any sales experience, but I was a competitor. I could set and crush goals, and I was eager to learn even more to benefit me in the long haul.

A family friend told me about a pharmaceutical company that was hiring a business development manager. I knew nothing about pharmaceutical sales, but I was eager and ready to devour the process. I perfected my cover letter and résumé, included my accomplishments and awards, and stressed my ability to set goals and not only compete for them but dominate them. I sent it to the director of HR, and within a week, I received the call for a formal interview. I had no idea what to expect, but I was confident. I had researched the company's mission statement and the position's specific requirements, and I was prepared to let them know why I was the only candidate they needed to consider. Nothing was going to stop me from winning these decision makers over.

After three successful rounds of interviews with the HR department, the regional director, and the vice president, I had an offer. It was a great job with a good starting salary, full benefits, vacation, everything people look for in their dream job. I was proud of myself. *I'm a business development manager for a reputable pharmaceutical company. Wow.* Though I had dreams of owning my own company one day, I was here to do the work at hand, and I knew it would only make my own future business better. I wanted to learn as much as I possibly could and add tremendous value to this company, as I promised the executives in my interviews. They told me they had never interviewed anyone with so much confidence and conviction, and they were eager to have me on board to help grow the company. Although this wasn't my dream job, I was present and ready to produce. I was thankful for the opportunity.

I, Matt Mayberry, joined the ranks of people who go to work every single day.

I needed to improve my skills in sales if I wanted to own

a successful business in the near future. If you can't sell your services, there won't be a business. Like everything I set out to do, I read every single sales book I could get my hands on, listened to every guru's audiotapes and online podcasts, and more.

TACKLE THIS TODAY

Sometimes you have to accept a job that you don't necessarily want to do in order to take care of yourself. You have to be responsible. It does not mean that you give up your dreams and goals. It just means that you work while you're simultaneously building the business that owns your heart and passion. No experience is ever wasted. Everything you do will contribute to the overall best in you.

I then went out into the real world as *Matt Mayberry, Business Development Manager*, and I put everything that I was learning into hands-on practice while on the job. I worked directly with Mark Vinson, the regional director. He took me right under his wing. We worked the upper Midwest region of Iowa, Illinois, Michigan, Wisconsin, and Indiana. Our sole focus was to grow the company throughout our region, getting our product in every nursing home, hospital, and care facility. I studied as much as possible and asked Mark every question I could think of. I pitched our product and services to owners, CEOs, and executives, and we began to grow the company throughout the Midwest.

For two years I worked as a business development manager in pharmaceutical sales, and this was also where I expanded my business IQ. I grew as an individual as well, and everything I was learning was of tremendous value to my life. I treated the position as an educational vehicle, and I could later apply all the principles, lessons, and strategies I learned to my future business endeavors. I don't think any of our experiences are ever wasted. There is a reason for everything, and even though I wasn't working at my dream job, it was an excellent stepping-stone for my purpose. I couldn't have asked for a better opportunity.

I learned something else. Being an athlete benefited me in many key areas, because I was willing to work long and hard hours to become the absolute best. There is nothing like sports training to make you competitive and teach you to constantly strive to become the best you can be.

All I had to do was recall that Coach Hep had told me I would be more successful outside of football than I would be on the field. I understood that I had to keep moving the ball down the field and score. No matter what I was doing in life, I had to *keep moving*. It was too important, and there was no way I wanted to slide back into that depraved, dark world.

Nelson Mandela once remarked that we do no one any favors "hiding our light" and pretending to be "smaller than we are."* But sometimes, because we might try to be modest, we will play small and stay small. We don't expect anything

---

* Quoted in Julia Cameron, *Walking in This World: The Practical Art of Creativity* (New York: Jeremy P. Tarcher / Penguin, 2002).

bigger of ourselves. And then we let fear and all those other negative things take over, and we stay small for the rest of our lives. Sure, it might be more comfortable to get a good job and stay there. There is nothing wrong with that if it fits you, your lifestyle, and your goals. But what I've learned is that most highly creative people have different songs in their hearts. And it is very difficult for us creative ones to play small for very long. We burst at the seams waiting to expand our possibilities and tap into our creative power.

If the universe has big plans for us, we are far better off if we cooperate instead of resist. And if we can surrender to becoming as large as we are meant to be—if we can embrace that golden enlightenment and awakening that we have felt—then great events and opportunities can and will come to pass for us and countless others.

Even though I felt like a failure because my public speaking career had taken a nosedive, I was not going to stop moving that ball. I knew that in life, Coach Hep would want me to Get Better Today and stop at nothing to achieve my goals.

I hated to be second best in anything, and I didn't want to be just another number or statistic. No matter how hard it was, I always wanted to stand out and dominate whatever it was I was doing at the time. So, I had to do that in sales, too.

Eventually I learned how to switch that same athletic mentality and energy over into the business world. I found that almost everything that helped propel me to the top as an athlete helped me soar to the top in sales and business, as well.

TACKLE THIS TODAY

Do not be afraid to reach out to others who have braved this path before you. Many successful people are more than happy to mentor you and give you advice to help you achieve your dreams and goals. They will gladly pay it forward, and when you do become successful, do not forget to pay it forward to some other young, aspiring person. You never know how grateful that person will be and how it will impact their lives forever.

I reached out to every successful motivational speaker, thought leader, and published author I could find. Some never responded while others wrote back and offered to help in any way they could. These giants included Stedman Graham, Jon Gordon, Matthew Kelly, and numerous others. I was—and still am—grateful for every single one of them, even the ones who couldn't help out but at least took the time to wish me the best of luck. I learned everything that I possibly could about writing and speaking while I was busy trying to be the best salesperson I could for the pharmaceutical company.

Out of all the different strategies and ideas that were shared with me, the one that worked the best and really gained some traction for me was: "Speak wherever you possibly can, even if it's for free and even if there are only three or ten people." It was called practice.

I made the rounds in Chicago and called local libraries, nonprofits, and community organizations and associations, and I asked if I could come and speak to their people. I inquired about their budgets, and if they told me they didn't have one, I offered to speak free of charge.

I swallowed my pride and ego and let go of all the pretentiousness that sometimes comes with being in the public. I simply didn't care how I was perceived or how few people attended. I was willing to speak whenever and wherever in between my time on the regular sales job.

Not only was I impacting others and making a difference, but I was getting better each time I spoke. My self-confidence increased. My heart got bigger while my bank account grew with each paycheck from my regular job.

My time consisted of going to work during the day, then coming home at night after a workout at the gym and directing all my energy and time toward speaking, studying, researching, and learning from mentors who had already made it to the top. I stayed up late watching videos of some of the best speakers in the world and visualizing myself up there onstage with them delivering my message and impacting millions of people.

TACKLE THIS TODAY

When trying to build a new career or achieve a new goal, don't be afraid to offer your services for free. You can always approach a company or a professional and ask if you can intern for them for free. This is an excellent way to learn the ropes of any job or career.

People have asked me if I had a social life during this time. I tell everyone the same thing: "No, I was too busy working on my dreams." Those dreams meant more to me than partying or anything else. I was so young and so full of energy and hope, and I wanted to become a successful public speaker and writer more than anything in the world.

THINGS YOU CAN TACKLE NOW TO UTILIZE THE DISCIPLINE OF ATHLETES IN ANY JOB

1. Hard work. Athletes are hard workers. They have to be. They not only train their physical bodies but their mental bodies. They learn how to work as a team as well as individually. So, tackle whatever you want to achieve with the mind-set of an athlete, and it will assist you in business, sports, education, and even in your personal life. The hard work will pay off.

2. Self-discipline. If you're going to train like an athlete, then you have to discipline your body and mind. You may have to roll out of bed in the early hours of the morning to tackle some task or exercise. You may hate the idea of this, but it's the self-discipline you need. You simply have to do things you don't want to do in order to get to where you want to be.

3. Accept losing. There will be times that no matter how hard you train or work, you will lose. You may work hard to sell a product. You may do your best to get a new client, but in the end, the client buys from another salesperson. You did everything you could possibly do. This does not mean you're a failure; it only means that someone else fits the client better. And if you fail in something, remember that it can be turned into a gift. You can learn from your failures. In sports, teams are always losing. Seldom does a team have a straight winning season. But when a team loses, they stop and analyze what they did wrong. They watch videos of their performances, and they study their playbooks. Failures can teach you what to do the next time so you will win. Losing is a fact of life, and it's best to just accept it and move on. Implement Coach Hep's "Get Better Today" motto and promise yourself you will keep on working hard. The positive attitude will bring about positive changes in your life.

4. Teamwork. Athletes who play team sports learn that the success of the individual is not as important as the success of the team. Honestly, this teaches players humility and selflessness. It also teaches them how to work well with others in order to achieve a common goal. You can apply this attitude in all your personal and business goals, and it will help you achieve them.

5. Do your best. No matter what you're doing, always, always do your best. When I spoke with Stedman at that youth leadership conference, I didn't prepare and do my best. Not really. I was too consumed with self-pity. But I have learned that you should always do your best. Thank goodness Stedman and others saw more in me and my abilities than I did. While doing your best, do not compare yourself with others. Remember that each person has particular talents and abilities that no one else has. Just do your best and you'll have nothing to feel embarrassed about.

I had spent most of my life watching films on other football teams or another linebacker who I wanted to emulate in my game, so I switched that athletic discipline and mentality over to becoming a speaker. I was officially a student again, and I never stopped learning. Even now, I try to learn something new each and every day.

Whether I was talking to a top athlete or a famous published author and public speaker, I found the one thing they had in common was their eagerness and drive to get better. "Get Better Today." There was Coach Hep's slogan again. It has stayed with me all my life. I have been completely amazed that all successful people practice GBT every day.

Looking back on it now, having the sales job was one of the greatest things that could have happened to me, because it gave me the time to scrutinize some of the best authors and public speakers in the world while I had stability. I devoured everything I could. I soaked it up like a sponge, because I was eager to learn from them and become the best myself. When I studied Jon Gordon, Matthew Kelly, Stedman Graham, and so many others and discovered what they did behind the scenes, I saw all the hard work that went into being the best. Holding a steady job gave me free time at night to absorb it all and then implement their wisdom into my own life and practice.

I also learned the importance of patience. When I first set out to write and speak full-time, I hadn't learned about paying my dues, and I wanted my new dreams and the world handed to me immediately. Many people who have big goals want instant gratification. They aren't willing to go to work at a job for years before ever seeing a return or payoff from the hard work they put in. It takes some longer than others. Some make it and some don't.

So many people put off their dreams out of fear or whatever, but they sometimes wait too long. Maybe they have their own plans and believe in "slow but sure." That's okay, too. We're all different. And I admit I can be quite impatient sometimes because my dreams are big and my spirit continues to grow larger and larger. I am simply not comfortable resting in yesterday's definition of myself.

I was busy reprogramming myself with all my studying and hard work, diligently trying to make myself whole again. I had no intention of being and staying small. My universe was simply too large.

Once we have experienced a serious failure, we're pretty much knocked to the ground. We have to reprogram the inner pathway and redirect ourselves to the desired destination. We have to reboot our faith into something bigger than ourselves, our awareness and inner strength. And we have to connect with positive and supportive family and friends and let them in on our reprogramming. When we do all this, we revolutionize our world.

Greatness doesn't happen overnight, and all the incredibly successful individuals I have ever met had to work for years without ever seeing much of a payoff. It taught me the importance of having a strategy in place, because without one there's no way you'll win in the long term. Oh, sure, you may get some success and traction in the beginning, but over time it's practically impossible to win without a strategy and a plan of action to *work* that strategy. In football, we developed strategies every single day, such as how we were going to perform in practice or how we were going to travel for an away game. There was always a plan of action for us to execute.

When you blindly go into something without a strategy, a disaster could be waiting around the corner. It's such a good analogy for a business. A start-up isn't going to secure investors without a business plan and a strategy that shows how it is unique, how much money it will earn, and how it's going to be successful. The same thing needs to happen for you.

I worked for two full years at a job I wasn't that crazy about in order to earn a steady paycheck. But while I was doing that, I learned everything I possibly could about how to grow and operate a successful business.

Meanwhile, some serious traction was starting to take place.

Keep in mind that during this time, I was willing to speak anywhere and everywhere and at times even for free. That eventually made me a better speaker, and it also built a buzz about my presentation and me as a public speaker. The better I got, the further the word spread. I was actually beginning to get paid handsomely to speak at sales conferences, executive meetings, and conferences all over the country.

While building this speaking career, I incorporated my own story into each presentation. I talked about my failures and how I learned that each failure was a gift because each one prompted me to get up and dust myself off and figure out what I was going to do next. But I also constantly looked for other impactful stories to share with my audiences and researched hours and hours of videos of high-performance speakers and success experts.

After a year and a half of public speaking, I had finally built a solid enough strategy and action plan to venture out on my own and leave my position as a business development manager.

Now I live my dream every single day of my life. From the ground up, failure after failure, gift after gift, a whole lot of perseverance, hard work, faith, and hope, I am writing and speaking all over the country full-time, and I am the happiest I have ever been.

Today, after each and every presentation I give, regardless of who or where the audience is, I well up with tears backstage or when I'm back in my hotel room. I simply can't hold back the emotion. I am so grateful, so humbled, so honored, to be living this dream. I think about the drugs, the people I hurt, my wins and losses as a football player, and then the ups and downs in between.

We can all have multiple destinies, because we're not limited by one or two things in our lives. I believed I was destined to be the best football player to ever live. While in sports, I never knew that football wasn't my true purpose or passion. I love the game, and it has brought many blessings into my life. It may have even saved my life. I have developed lifelong friendships from the game, and for that I'm grateful.

But looking back, I realize that football was only a detour to lead me to my real purpose.

If you feel that your life isn't whole or that you aren't living a purpose-driven life, let my story be a light of hope for you. Let your failures be gifts that direct you to where you need to be—to a place that's big enough to hold your big spirit. We are all a divine spark of something greater—a shining, bright, burning candle intended to light our path and that of our fellow travelers.

When I think of bright candles, fellow travelers, and big spirits, I can't help but think of two of the most important people who have been in my life: Grampa Dee and Coach Hep. Grampa Dee passed away a few years ago. I think about him and Coach Hep all the time, and I miss them every day. I know they're with me through every failure, every success, every dream. I can hear Grampa Dee telling me when I was a little boy out on the ball field, "Matt, you are very special and I know you're going to grow up to be great." And I can hear Coach Hep right behind him saying, "You *will excel* on the field, but you will become more successful *outside* of football than you ever are *in* football." And, of course, I hear his most famous motto of all: "Get Better Today."

I encourage all of you to find the bravery to dream again and rediscover the parts of yourselves that have been misplaced and forgotten. Let yourself open up to your own divine spark and follow that light. You are not small. You are large and beautiful, and there is a whole new world waiting for you. Just remember to leave the door open a little bit… a tiny crack…so the light can get in.

YOUR OWN PERSONAL GAME PLAN
TO PUT INTO ACTION

1. Relentless. Be relentless in your pursuit to achieve your dreams and goals. The last thing I wanted to do was get a job. I worried about what others would think of me. I worried that I would look like a big fool. Here I had decided to not play football again with ambitious plans to embark on a new journey, and then right when I thought everything was going smoothly, I fell flat on my face and had to take a job to pay the bills. Weeks into the job, it dawned on me how many people put so much energy into complaining and focusing on the negative instead of directing that energy toward achieving their dreams. Everyone has an enormous dream, but why is it that so few people actually make that dream a reality? I was willing to show up to work every morning, because I knew that one day in the near future that job would help me get to where I wanted to go. I was relentless in my efforts to learn all I could about sales so I could apply the knowledge to my public speaking career when the time came. In order for your biggest goals and dreams to become a reality, you must be willing to do whatever it takes to get the job done. Even jobs that aren't exciting or fun. It's all about paying the price and sacrificing short-term pleasure for long-term satisfaction and gain. Not to mention, when you possess this type of mental attitude and willingness to fight for your dream, you'll be that much stronger and more prepared to become successful.

2. The genius of mentorship. When I first failed at starting a successful public speaking and writing business, I knew I needed to learn from those who were already succeeding at it. I strongly believe that having an experienced and willing mentor will do more for your personal and professional life than any book, any online course, or any other type of learning material available. I wouldn't be where I am right now if it wasn't for the guidance of all the incredible mentors I have had over the years. Without their assistance, I'm not quite sure that I would have been able to build my speaking business and writing career at all. Here are a few extra thoughts on finding a great mentor or friend to help you:

- It's important to think big from the start! If you can't picture yourself being successful and living your dream, then you will have a very hard time attracting the great men and women who can and will help you.

- Be realistic and recognize that you don't know everything. Acting like a know-it-all or being egotistical is one of the best ways to ensure that you won't find the mentor you're seeking.

- Don't ever forget to trust your intuition and instincts. This is your passion, your business, and your life. It's very important to listen to advice, but also be careful to filter it. No one, even a great mentor, is in charge of your life and your decisions. Stay true to yourself.

- No one will have all the answers; however, a great mentor can help you find the answers for yourself or put you in touch with someone who can help.

- Always think in terms of value. Constantly look for ways that you can add value to your mentor. If they agree to mentor you, they are giving you one of their most prized possessions—their time. Before I would even think twice about reaching out to a mentor, I would research what current projects they were working on, their books, and their websites to see how I could add value to them.

- Find different mentors for different areas of your life and business. I have a mentor for almost every area of my life. Plus, I have three mentors for different aspects of my business.

- Application will always be king! Learning from a mentor will do absolutely nothing if you don't take action and actually apply what you have learned. Once you have a mentor who is willing to invest in you and help out, it's imperative that you take action.

Chapter Twelve

WINNING PLAYS TO TURN *FAILURE* INTO A GIFT

The most visible joy can only reveal itself to us when we've transformed it, within.

—*Rainer Maria Rilke*

Experiences of all kinds can awaken the soul to something greater than ourselves. To greater stories, to greater possibilities. I believe that generally the stories we end up telling others are our authentic stories about ourselves. The ones that come straight from our hearts. Because, after all, we're storytellers and we want to know that others care about our stories, too. It makes us whole.

It may be a while before you pay attention to your own stories and what they say about you. That's okay. Take all the time you need. Once you understand your story and share it with others, you will use it to more actively become the author of your own life and the creator of unlimited possibilities. For in those possibilities lie the gifts that are waiting for you at every turn.

It's my hope that you've been able to take away something valuable from my crazy roller-coaster ride of a story. My topsy-turvy journey that has led me through failures and comebacks. Negatives and positives. Despairs and awakenings. Losing plays and winning plays. I hope both my bad and good experiences can help you understand your own as you navigate this world.

In this chapter, I have summarized a proven seven-step formula that will help you overcome failures and setbacks—losing plays and winning plays—in your life and turn those into golden gifts. This formula won't make the pain sting any less, but it may provide a little comfort if you can analyze failure and understand its purpose.

I created this formula after reflecting on failure one night and wondering how I overcame each setback. Was it a fluke? Was it a bit of magic that zapped me from somewhere? Or was it a gift from God? Maybe you're thinking it was from all these things. One thing is for sure: There were times when I didn't think I'd ever get out of the darkness. When I didn't think I'd ever find that crack where the light poured in.

Throughout my life, I have studied other men and women, mainly highly successful people who overcame tragic events and continued to live remarkable lives. Some of them are now my friends, my mentors. During my research, I discovered a pattern. They all utilized the same kinds of principles and philosophies to overcome their failures and turn them into gifts the way I did. I discovered plenty of formulas about how to achieve success, but I didn't find a concrete hands-on formula for how to overcome failure. How to power through and continuously dominate when you're experiencing the worst of times.

When I've studied other successful people, I've noticed that most assuredly they had setbacks. In fact, I believe everyone has and will continue to have setbacks, failures, roadblocks, and hardships. Myself included. I know it and I'm ever vigilant, ready to tackle the challenges that come my way. Because it's just a part of life.

My overall studies and analyses prompted me to create something that would stick and resonate with others, so I took the word *failure* and broke it down into an acronym. In FAILURE, each letter stands for a strength that resulted from my failures and in turn became multiple gifts. This formula is based on personal experiences, even scientific research, along with spiritual and biblical principles.

TACKLE THIS TODAY

When you are at the end of your rope and believe you have nothing to offer this world, stop and remember that faith can carry you through life and make the difficulties easier to bear. We are all a divine spark of God. We are all brilliant with light. We are all beautiful souls. We just forget sometimes.

It is my hope that no matter how hard your life is—no matter how many failures you experience—this formula can serve as a tool and a guiding light to illuminate the path before you, just as it has in mine and thousands of others who have applied it.

The best way to put this formula into practice in your own life is simple. The next time you feel discouraged, stuck, or defeated, read through each of the seven letters in FAILURE and rate yourself on a scale from one to ten where you stand with each one. In fact, write these letters down on an index card and carry it in your briefcase, purse, or wallet.

Let's review the letters and see how you can apply them to your own situation. The key to reaping the most rewards is to make sure you apply each letter in synchrony. The synergistic power of each letter will work together to provide a stronger basis for you to turn your failures into a gift. You won't see as many results if you focus on only one or two letters and neglect the others.

Is this formula easy to follow and apply when you have failed at something or are going through a difficult patch? Absolutely not. But think about it. What worthwhile thing in life is ever easy?

F *Stands for "Faith"*

The first letter in FAILURE is *F*, which stands for "Faith." When examining what it takes to become all that you can be and turn any failure or adversity in your life into an incredible gift, faith is an excellent starting point. I know faith is the reason I have prevailed after every failure. Let me explain further.

When I reflect on my own journey and recall the hundreds

of conversations I have had with high achievers and maximum performers from around the world and all different walks of life, faith was always a topic of discussion. These thought leaders explained how they got to where they *are* from where they *were*, and all of them discussed the power of their faith in a higher power. They believed in something greater than themselves.

Faith can mean a lot of things, and in this context, I am referring to having faith in something much bigger than yourself. If you can keep this faith with you and trust that there is a larger purpose for your life than whatever failure or tribulation you're undergoing, then you already own a strong tool to turn that failure into a gift.

This is the spectacular thing about faith. It's ongoing. It's not about instant gratification, although there can be an instant peace of mind. My circumstances didn't change the moment I cried for God's help. I had to be reminded— the hard way—that life is not about instant gratification or reward but about the journey. It's about having faith in life's redirections and its detours, and trusting the process. I had to remember that God is not a genie. He doesn't go "Abra-cadabra" and grant wishes. However, He *will* provide you with a moral compass and the tools you need to fulfill your voyage if you follow His will.

Our moral compass is faith's backbone. The foundation of all that we are. It will carry us and guide us on our journey and may be one of the most important tools there is.

What happened when I called God back into my life was something that I had not done for such a long time. And what I received was something I hadn't felt in a long time:

clarity and peace of mind. I felt as though a tremendous burden had been lifted from my shoulders as I released years of bottled-up pain, hatred, and emotions. I surrendered to this higher power, understanding that He, who was so much greater than me, needed to be at the forefront of my life every single day if I ever planned on making something of myself. There was a long, difficult road ahead, but I was willing to trust the process. I had renewed faith. I was fully on board. And I tackled my redirection—my God-given purpose in life—with a zest and a passion like never before.

What I learned at age sixteen was that without faith, we are absolutely nothing. I know this as a definite truth because I have lived without it, and I also have lived with it, and life is just so much smoother when we live with it. When it's at the forefront of our everyday life and every decision we make.

I understand that this may not ring true for everyone. You may have a different perspective or definition of this thing that's bigger than you. And that's all right. This is what I have learned to be true for myself and many others. Each of us has a different story, and that's the beauty of it all.

TACKLE THIS TODAY

Do you have faith in something bigger than yourself? Do you stop and listen for the quiet? Do you stop and go within to talk to God? Do you hear the answers?

Having faith in something bigger than ourselves sets us on a whole new path of enlightenment when we are broken-hearted and our spirits are crushed. It shines a light on our world when we are going through complete darkness and think there's no way out.

In the previous years, before my breakdown at age sixteen, I had never relied on my faith to get me through the depressing times or as a way to pick myself back up after a failure. I just relied on a drug to give me a high. That was my escape. That was why I always found myself going round and round in the same circle, never getting better or moving forward. I was stuck. Lost. Closed off from the light. And it was not a good place.

I have learned that all great achievements in this world came from people who had enormous faith in not only themselves but in the possibilities for their life and future. They hung on to this faith when they faced uncertainty and tough times. Just like everything in life, we have choices to make regarding how we live. Are we going to wallow in our failures and cry, "Oh, poor, poor me!" Or are we going to rise above them and use our faith to trust and believe that we can be more?

The decision is ours alone. We must take initiative early on and vow to do everything in our power to destroy our fears, learn from our failures, understand and embrace the gifts from each failure, and live according to our faith. The more we experience failures, especially large failures, the more our fears will creep into our lives and try to rob us of our peace and happiness.

Interestingly enough, fear, failure, and faith have a lot in common to an extent. I call them the Big Three. When we fail at something, we let fear stop us from trying again, and that overrides our faith. And when we operate out of fear because of our failures, we put belief into a future that is unwritten and totally without faith. It is up to each of us to write our own future, our own story. I, for one, want to make it a great one and will always include faith in my story.

Faith focuses on the positive while fear focuses on the negative. When people experience a setback or a failure, they immediately assume there is no choice but to accept the outcome of that failure. They lose sight of the fact that the first step in conquering failure and uncovering the gift is to constantly develop and strengthen the faith muscle, which will help them destroy their fears and try again.

When bad things happened to me and failure came knocking, I activated my fears and not my faith. *I took more drugs!* It wasn't until I hit rock bottom after going to rehab that I truly understood the importance of never focusing on my fears again. Sure, I believe it's important to acknowledge your fears, but then you must let them go. Crush them. Destroy them.

When I realized that each failure gave me the opportunity to learn—to find the gift, the gold—and to grow from the experience, I understood that faith was the carrier of the moral compass that would transport me to an enlightened state, and at times, a complete reawakening.

At the end of the day, you can't live in both fear and faith. It's one or the other. Whichever one you choose will immediately drive out the other from your life, and the result will be a new creation of your story.

A *Stands for "Analyze"*

The second letter in our acronym is *A* for "Analyze." It simply means stopping and taking the time to think. It means using discipline to tune out distractions and diagnose the situation at hand. What do you need to do to change things? To improve your life? To overcome a certain problem? Stop. Think. Analyze.

Think of the last time you failed or experienced a setback that seemed to shatter your entire world. What was going through your mind at the time? I bet it was a rush of negative thoughts questioning your ability to get the job done or wondering if you had the talent to achieve something.

One of the major mistakes most people make is to let the overflow of negative thoughts steer them in a direction that leads them down a path toward self-destruction. When we are excited about something and temporarily fail or experience an outcome that we weren't expecting, we find reasons to justify why we weren't worthy, good enough, or capable of accomplishing it in the first place. We live in a noisy and distracting world, especially in the heightened technology-driven era we're in right now. People don't stop and listen to their thoughts. Nowadays, they don't stop much to actually talk to one another, either. Everything is communicated via texts, e-mails, and social media outlets. Ever notice people out having dinner together and how one or two of them are talking on their cell phone or texting? If people can't even relate to each other, how can they relate to themselves?

The whole point is that we have to stop and *think*.

TACKLE THIS TODAY

When you meet friends for dinner or coffee, do you find yourself texting on your phone and excluding them from the conversation? Do you have a habit of taking your iPad with you everywhere you go so you can check news sites online? Do you sometimes play games on your smartphone while visiting with your family? Do you use so much technology in your life that you have totally forgotten how to unplug and think?

In times of despair and helplessness, the last thing you want to think about is what you're experiencing or how to actually resolve the issue. But it's important to stop and analyze it and figure out what's not working and how you can change it.

For many years of my life, I always rushed to a judgment and declared the absolute worst about a situation without ever taking the proper time to fully analyze it. To give you a perfect example, when I didn't get drafted in the NFL on Draft Day, I believed my life was over. I was miserable and thought it was the worst day of my life. My world came crashing down on me for a while, but after I signed a free agent contract with the Chicago Bears, I pushed the disappointment away and analyzed the situation. What I had deemed as a major failure was actually a blessing in disguise. If another team had drafted me, I wouldn't have had the chance to play for the Chicago Bears, the hometown team I loved to watch as a kid. Everything has a reason and a purpose. The tough times, the disappointments, and the setbacks are all designed to teach us something about ourselves.

I can ramble on and on about many similar scenarios when I was quick to rush to judgment and had thought the absolute worst was happening. I'm learning not to do that anymore. The key word here is *learning*. It's always a process. We learn things, but that doesn't mean we'll never have a failure again. We must keep reinforcing those things we learned every day and implement them into our lives when times get tough.

The next time you go through a tough personal or business matter, stop and analyze the situation that feels negative, even heartbreaking. Try talking to trusted mentors, parents, accountability partners, friends, and anyone else who will have an unbiased point of view. Sometimes all we need is another perspective when we're feeling down and our self-confidence is low.

The reason many people never overcome their failures or build upon their adversities is because they don't analyze the situation and come up with solutions. Most people seem quick to think the worst after a failure. When people are too judgmental too quickly, they can compound the problem. Organizations do the same thing. When individuals and organizations focus on solutions, not more problems, they are able to grow after tremendous setbacks and actually get better because of them.

> ## TACKLE THIS TODAY
>
> Do you understand how failures can be a blessing in disguise? Take a look at your life and all the failures and setbacks you have endured. Can you identify the blessings and gifts that came into your life as a result of these setbacks?

Thomas Edison's persistence and eagerness to continually search for solutions despite facing one failure after another is an incredible example of the significance of focusing on advancement. Failure is never a final destination or an end result unless you make it so. Edison used every experience, failure, and attempt to move him one step closer to his goals. This is the same type of mind-set we need to apply to our own lives and businesses when failure and adversity arise. We have to remember that what we focus on *expands*. If we focus only on our problems and failures, then that's exactly what we will get more of. If we focus on solutions and take the proper time to analyze everything that is going on, we will begin to receive more signals on how to move forward. And therein lies the gift.

I *Stands for "Increase"*

The third letter in our acronym is *I* for "Increase." One of Failure's best friends is Decrease. Mr. Decrease shows up every time we encounter a difficulty. Think about it for a second. What did you do the last time a hardship happened unexpectedly? If you are part of a very small percentage of people, you kept going, you kept fighting, and you kept advancing. You increased your personal power and moved forward fast and hard.

But if you are like a great majority of the population, you let Mr. Decrease waltz into your life and take over. He convinced you to play small instead, to forget how large you really are. To *decrease* your belief in yourself. He charmingly seduced you into believing that there's little left for you in life and that you have no personal power whatsoever.

It's nearly impossible to be great and achieve your biggest goals and dreams if you aren't thinking big and taking massive action toward that goal. You certainly aren't turning failure into a gift if you play the victim and let Mr. Decrease become your new best friend.

Most of us are affected mentally, physically, and emotionally when failure hits, especially if it's severe and life-altering. Some may know how to handle the tough times better than others, but failure can paralyze us if we don't increase the positive actions and thoughts in our lives.

Keep in mind that we don't just want to *overcome* failure; we want to truly learn from it and turn it into a gift. We want to become better *because* of that adversity and hardship. In order to do that, we need to increase everything we are and everything we do. And when I say increase everything, I mean *everything*. *Increase* your personal power, positivity, attitude of gratitude, physical strength, health and fitness, intelligence, the action you're taking, the quality of your relationships, and your relationship with faith. Increase *everything* in you to become the best you can be. Mr. Decrease won't stand a chance.

TACKLE THIS TODAY

Are you buying into the notion that life is dreary and difficult and something to plod through without any real happiness or zest? It's up to you to reclaim your God-given right to flourish in life by increasing every part of yourself.

Through some of the biggest disappointments in my life I have also found some of the biggest blessings and gifts. There is a personal power that can sometimes tie us to the disappointments. If we let it, it will completely change the direction of our lives and prohibit us from achieving our dreams. If we don't overcome our decreases, we'll never be able to focus on the increases. That means doing all we can to increase our personal power and stand tall in the fight to improve our lives.

The one thing I can promise you is that there are multiple blessings and gifts waiting for you behind your biggest disappointments. I didn't know at the time exactly what I was doing when I spoke at that youth leadership event with Stedman Graham after I was injured, but that was when I discovered the power of increasing my actions so positive influences could start coming into my life. If we don't take initiative on changing our state of being and our attitude when we get knocked to the ground, then life will do that for us automatically.

The increase method is an integral part of tackling adversity and achieving lasting success that fulfills you for a lifetime. You aren't like the rest of the population, and there isn't anything ordinary about you. Don't let failure dictate your destiny and achievement levels. When you are intentional about it, the increase method will eventually become a natural way of doing things. While most will continue to play small and do enough to just get by, they might be amazed at all the incredible things you're doing in the world despite what you've had to overcome. Remember to increase and not decrease. Become more of who you already are, and kick Mr. Decrease to the curb.

L *Stands for "Lead"*

The fourth letter in the acronym and the fourth process to turn failure into a gift is *L* for "Lead." When I talk about "leading," I am referring to being the leader of your destiny. Of your life. Being your own CEO. I'm talking about taking complete responsibility for your life and not blaming others or your circumstances for past results or where you are right now.

Mind you, every single one of these seven letters that define a process in the acronym FAILURE is vitally important, but if you aren't willing to lead your life and be the CEO of your destiny, nothing else in this book will work.

Why is it that someone can go year after year, month after

month, and day after day complaining about the laundry list of misfortunes in their life but then do absolutely nothing about it? It's always been mind-boggling to try and wrap my head around this. I hear so many people say they want to be great, achieve more success, and make more money. But they never do anything about it. The only thing these people do is whine and complain about their sorry lot in life. They sit back and let others make their decisions.

Granted, I understand there are situations and issues in people's lives that may prevent them from achieving their dreams. There can be circumstances that are beyond their control. Families, disabilities, illnesses, to name a few. I'm not judging people when I see them living in undesirable situations, because I know that it's possible life has dealt them a bad hand and they can't navigate their way out. I get it, and I do not mean to sound preachy.

On the flip side, I see others who *could do* something about their lives if they tried. I've seen people go through very challenging times, even worse than my own. But some simply make excuses as to why they're currently where they are.

"I don't have any talent."

"I can't ever seem to get a good job. Someone better always gets the job."

"I can't make enough money to pay my bills."

"I don't have any luck at all."

Does this sound like anyone you know? They make you want to kick them in the butt and say, "Stop feeling sorry for yourself! You can change your destiny! You can change your life!"

Nike's slogan "Just Do It!" has been one of the best in the advertising world. Getting up off your butt and going out there and achieving something is the way you become the leader of your life.

Sure, I know. I agree with you. I've been through it, so I'm speaking from experience. One of the hardest things to do is take full charge of your life and be the leader of your destiny. But when you do, you are forcing yourself to look at your life and say, "I am not where I want to be *because of myself* and the past choices and decisions that I have made." Your next comment may be, "I am going to do something about it and make a positive change."

When you do this, you're taking ownership for where you are and where you are headed. And that's not an easy thing to do, trust me. One of the hardest things I ever did was force myself to look *within* when times were not the best. Heck, I could barely look at myself in the mirror. I was so despicable. But when I truly looked in the mirror and then looked within and surrendered to my faith, things began to change. Slowly but surely, I became the CEO of my life. The leader of my destiny.

TACKLE THIS TODAY

If you keep blaming everyone else for your situation, you will never become the leader of your life. You will never know what it is to be your own CEO. What can you do today to ensure you are the leader and CEO of your world?

When I thought about becoming my own leader, this redefined my philosophy of life. It will redefine yours, as well. When you choose to be the CEO of your life, there is absolutely nothing you can't do or overcome. Being the leader of your destiny is rejecting the easy road and opting for what's worth it in the long run.

Think about it. It would be a shame if you got to the final stages of your life and all you had to account for were your excuses for why you didn't follow a passion or a dream. It breaks my heart to even think about this, but it happens all the time.

Becoming the leader of your destiny opens the floodgates of opportunity, and life seems to become a bit easier, because others will join in and help when they can.

For example, let's say there are two young men named John and Chris. John is the leader of his destiny. When something goes wrong, he doesn't make excuses or place the blame on someone else. John doesn't focus on the negative. He constantly searches for ways to better himself and elevate his position in life.

Chris is a totally different story. He has a long track record of letting his failures define him. Every chance he gets, he makes excuses or blames someone else for his misfortunes and lack of success. It truly is a negative, energy-draining experience for anyone who comes in contact with him.

Out of the two men, who do you think is more likely to receive more opportunities to get back on the right track and have others want to help in any way they can? The answer to that question is obvious. People gravitate toward positive people. They're attractive and make you feel good. On the other hand, it's difficult to be around negative people because they're a liability to your happiness.

One of the most rewarding decisions you can ever make is to become the leader of your destiny, your own CEO, and take complete responsibility for everything that happens. Once you do, it won't be long before your opportunities begin to expand. And others will go out of their way to help you, even if it's something simple. Being the leader of your destiny is a trait that all champions possess.

U *Stands for "Unite"*

The next letter in the acronym for recognizing the gift in FAILURE is *U* for "Unite." The people you surround yourself with—the people you *unite* with—will bring out either the best or the worst in you.

If I followed you around for an entire week and paid very close attention to your relationships, I could tell a lot about your life and where you're headed. You may not necessarily agree with me, but the impact our relationships have on the quality of our lives and achievement levels is extraordinary.

Most important, whom we unite with when we're knocked down by failure and adversity influences how we overcome it and if we can turn it into a gift. Point out successful people who have overcome a great deal of setbacks throughout the course of their lifetimes, and I can guarantee they have strong, supportive, growth-oriented relationships. And in general, among those relationships, the people will be like-minded with similar moral compasses and belief systems.

Our network of friends and family can impact our lives. I know this all too well, because I have been on both sides of the fence. As I discussed earlier, some of the darkest moments of my life were because of the group of individuals I hung out with when I was a teenager. Not only did this group stir up mischievous, even criminal, behavior everywhere they went, but they promoted mediocrity in each other. They didn't strive to be anything bigger than what they were: partying druggies. They had no goals, no dreams, no ambitions. And they pulled me down into the gutter with them. I had united with the wrong group of friends, and for a while, I lost sight of what was possible for my life. I gave up any hope that I was going to be a success one day.

TACKLE THIS TODAY

Be careful and selective when choosing friends and business associates to unite with. The good ones will uplift you and bring out the best in you, and the bad ones will bring you down and limit your abilities to grow and develop your full potential. Take a look around you. Who do you see?

Instead of uniting with athletes and other friends in high school who were positive, uplifting, and moving toward being the CEOs of their own lives someday, I chose the group who could give me a quick high and make me feel important. This gang had mediocre minds and bad attitudes, and they rubbed off on me. Teens are very impressionable, and I was one of them.

I wasn't raised like this. My parents and grandparents

were the antithesis of these wild kids who just wanted to party and get high. Gratefully, I was able to overcome that experience due to my faith and my strong family support system. I know it can be much more difficult for those who do not have a strong family to support them.

I have been blessed to reach extraordinary heights of success, expand my vision, and constantly be challenged to be better and do better all because of who I have been uniting with. This group of individuals, as you can imagine, is much different from the group of drug addicts I partied with. The friends, teachers, coaches, former teammates, mentors, and family I surround myself with today are supportive of all that I aspire to be. They never want to see me settle for anything less than what I deserve. And I am forever grateful.

As human beings, we all are naturally self-centered for the most part, some of us more than others. One of the reasons why so many people settle for an average inner circle of associates and friends who never challenge them to be better or push past their comfort zone is because their egos constantly need stroking. They only want to hear yes from the people around them. It is so tragic that men and women of all ages, from all demographics, and from every ethnicity go to their graves with their full potential still buried inside them because they listened to the yes-men who never held them accountable for their actions and never challenged them to be better. They united with the wrong kind of people and never broke free.

If you are in a rough spot in life, the last thing you need is someone telling you what you want to hear just to appease you. Instead, you absolutely need to hear those difficult truths.

And for most people, that's a very tough thing to deal with, especially if they're in denial about it. It doesn't feel good when someone says, "Get off your butt and get a job." Or "Your relationships are like poison to your potential. You need to do something about that." But we need a panel of trusted critics. We need that accountability. We need to hear these difficult truths, as they are necessary for our growth.

When I was a drug addict, I didn't want to hear that I needed to go to a drug treatment facility. *Me? No way.* But it was exactly what I needed to hear.

When I was a rookie with the Chicago Bears, they had special classes to teach us the ins and outs of being a pro football player. For many, life as a pro is a major adjustment. Some of the athletes arrive from situations where they were barely able to survive financially, and some come with struggles to support their families. But all of a sudden, the athletes sign big contracts and get lots of money. All of a sudden, they can afford to live a lavish lifestyle they had only dreamed of before.

One of the courses we participated in was about our surroundings and our circle of friends—who we united with—when making financial decisions. We were warned about the yes-men who would appear out of the woodwork now that we had made it.

Our advisers cited several examples of players who burned through incredible amounts of money and eventually filed for bankruptcy because of so-called friends and family members who waited around holding their hands out once the athletes made it big. These were people who were around for all the glory but dispersed quickly when the well ran dry. Rather than an entourage of yes-men, what these athletes needed were people to tell them the hard truths of their spending habits and about making conscious decisions for their money over the long haul. "Hey, the NFL won't last forever." Or "You may want to scale back on the extravagant lifestyle." I know it's difficult listening to things we don't want to hear from people who hold us accountable. Yet failing to do so is detrimental to our success in all areas of our lives.

The above example applies to every walk of life. You don't have to be a professional athlete to have yes-men in your life. They are everywhere. The last thing you want when you experience a failure is a weak-minded person who tries to latch on to you or unite with you in any area of life.

When people truly care for you and your well-being, they will want to be a trusted friend and confidant and be supportive, but they will tell you the truth. Even if it's a hard truth.

In the game of football, it takes an entire team to come together and overcome adversity, win games, and hopefully win championships. It takes a united front. Of course, there will always be a few star players on every team, but without each team member contributing and doing their best job, none of that happens. The same goes for all sports and work cultures.

In the business world, the exact same principle applies. Whether it's a small business or a Fortune 500 company, everyone needs to play his or her part in order to achieve any kind of success. They have to unite to create success.

That goes for the management team all the way down to the administrative assistants and custodians. That's the beautiful thing about a team. You are not alone. Just as your favorite sport includes their team members, why not create a team for yourself for one of the hardest sports of them all—the marathon of life?

Create a winning team around you, unite the best of the best—those you admire and want to emulate and who will push you to be better than you ever dreamed—and no failure will be able to hold you back!

R *Stands for "Reprogram"*

R is the sixth letter in our acronym, and it stands for "Reprogram." Just as with everything in life, we can choose either to limit our potential and let a past failure determine our destiny or to stand up to failure, despite what challenges come our way. When we're knocked down, we just have to get up, dust ourselves off, and reprogram our lives to get going and do something else.

Nothing has the potential to affect us in a negative way mentally, physically, or spiritually more than failure or hardship. Most people hate to fail so much that they don't even dream new dreams or go after what they truly desire. The fear of failure paralyzes their every move. They forget what it's like to actually live life. Instead, they choose to live their fears.

One of the major reasons why so many have a hard time reaching the mountaintop and creating breakthroughs is their inability to grow as a result of a failure. The growth may involve a complete reprogramming of yourself and your skills. It may mean you need more education, new skills, training, study, research, or mentoring to help you take a new direction. It may mean working jobs that are boring or that you're not crazy about to pay the bills while you pursue your true dreams and goals. Some people don't know how to do it, and some aren't willing.

So many people will never get the opportunity to turn failure into a gift because they haven't discovered the incredible benefits of getting better or reprogramming as a way to reboot, rekindle that fire within, and improve. As Coach Hep said, "Get Better Today." This motto will help you stay focused when you reprogram your life.

TACKLE THIS TODAY

Are you doing anything today to get better? Keep Coach Hep's GBT motto with you, and each morning make a list of things you can do to get better. Make a list of how these things will help you reprogram your life so you can achieve your dreams.

Let's look at some specific steps you can take to reprogram your life. The main goal should be to become so mentally, physically, and spiritually strong that virtually nothing can break you completely. And one way to do this is to reprogram your attitude.

THINGS YOU CAN TACKLE NOW TO REPROGRAM YOUR ATTITUDE TO ONE OF GRATITUDE

Many, many people talk about attitude and especially the "attitude of gratitude." It has become such a normal topic of discussion that few people probably really think about it. I'm not sure how many people actually work on their attitude daily. But trust me, it can make all the difference when it comes to reprogramming your life so you can reap the rewards and gifts of failure. It's important to have an attitude of gratitude and be grateful for everything in your life. Even—especially—the failures.

How can some people defeat the odds and achieve success? How can some turn major failures into incredible gifts that not only bless themselves but the entire world? Simple. It's the attitude they choose.

When our attitude is right, we can achieve maximum results. The right attitude can help us soar to greater heights than ever before and create extraordinary lives and businesses. Likewise, the right attitude can bring out the best in others. That's why I mentioned that we need to unite with people who have positive attitudes, because they will help us achieve our best.

You're probably saying, "This sounds great and all, but how am I ever supposed to have such a positive attitude when everything seems to be going wrong in my life?" I get it. I really do. It's still something I battle in my own life. Here are three simple ways to help you keep a positive attitude regardless of negative situations or events that present themselves throughout your journey.

1. Conscious effort. Make a deliberate effort to work on your attitude. I always heard about the importance of a great attitude, and every football coach I ever had brought it up, but I never really saw the value of it until I hit rock bottom. I struggled so much to keep a positive and encouraging attitude amid the failure and hard times, but that all changed when I finally made a conscious effort to improve my attitude despite what was going on in my life. Nothing will change if you don't change. Don't let circumstances or misfortunes dictate your attitude. Decide today to build up your attitude and attract the right kind of people into your life from here on out.

2. Affirmation card. Writing an attitude affirmation card can be a total game changer for you when you're rewiring and reprogramming your thinking. You can create an attitude shift for the better. I have always reaped tremendous benefits of "speaking things into existence" by repeating affirmations over and over, and the same goes for when I needed a change in my own attitude. When I wanted a Division I college scholarship, I wrote and recited every day, "I will receive a Division I scholarship," and it came true. Simply take out an index card and describe the exact type of attitude you want to possess. You can write something like, "I, [your name], am an honest, loving, and hardworking individual. I have a positive attitude, and I build up others and let my words radiate encouragement and success. No matter what happens in life, my attitude will never be sour and negative." This is just an example to help get you started, but you get the idea. We need to rewire and reprogram our thinking and declare the exact type of attitude we want. If we don't, it will be extremely hard to change our attitude when we experience a failure or a setback.

3. Goodness. Most poor attitudes stem from your perception of something, so start to look for the good in everyone and everything you come in contact with. If you look for the positive, your attitude will reflect that. An amazing transformation takes place when you see the good in everyone and everything, even failure.

Don't let a poor attitude be the reason why you stay in a mediocre state forever, why you never fulfill your potential, or why you never reprogram your life.

THINGS YOU CAN TACKLE NOW TO REPROGRAM YOUR MIND

Our mind is one of the most powerful tools we have. The process of reprogramming yourself starts in the mind, whether it is to earn a certain amount of money, kick an addiction, or overcome a particular tragedy. With that being said, most people overlook this powerful tool.

How have you used your intellect up to this point? Where you are right now, the amount of money you earn, how many failures you have turned into gifts, and the amount of satisfaction and happiness you have are all the results of past thinking.

You can either use your mind as an extremely powerful tool that will provide you with everything you need to make life a worthwhile adventure, or you can let your mind be your greatest enemy. You can let your mind tell you, *You cannot start over. You cannot reprogram yourself for anything else. You're stuck where you are.*

When failure occurs in your life, one of the very first things to be affected is your mind and the way you think. I'll never forget what some of the biggest failures I've endured did to my psyche. Not only did I start to see myself as "less than," but I began to doubt my self-worth and confidence. I viewed myself as a complete failure. A loser. I let my mind reinforce these thoughts constantly. I was probably harder on myself than anyone else.

I am not the only person who battles with keeping a positive, empowering, and uplifting mind-set when failure or tragedy strikes. It's something everyone experiences at one point or another.

Negativity is prevalent everywhere in life. We live in a negative world. We are wired to focus on the negatives, and we pay far too much attention to the hardships and failures.

Here are some steps to help you reprogram your mind:

1. Create and expand a beautiful vision. Oprah Winfrey reportedly said, "Create the highest, grandest vision for your life, because you become what you believe." You must envision this or it will never happen. See yourself as a champion. A victor. If you can't see it, you'll never achieve it. To help you do this, create a vision board or a notebook. Cut out pictures of the way you'd like to look, the life you'd like to live, words and mottos to reinforce your vision. This will help reprogram your life and attitude.

2. Reflect on life. What do you want your life to stand for? How do you want to be remembered? What do you want to contribute to the world? These are just three of life's biggest questions. By asking ourselves these intimate and extremely impactful questions, we get that much closer to living a life with purpose. Unfortunately, many men and women just coast along, never really taking the time to even think about life's biggest questions, let alone answer them. This causes them to move farther away from what ignites them so they can do meaningful work. Find what tugs at your heart and how you want to live. Those who neglect pondering and answering some of life's biggest questions will always struggle with adopting a winning and healthy mind-set, especially when disaster strikes.

3. Make yourself a trigger card. I call it a trigger card because one glance at this note card should have you fired up and ready to take things to the next level. It consists of writing your two most important goals on a note card. On the flip side of the card, pick two or three quotes that really move and inspire you. Whenever you are feeling unmotivated or down on your luck, pull your trigger card out and read it through a few times.

4. Read good, positive books. One of my favorites is *Mindset: The New Psychology of Success.* This is a phenomenal book by world-renowned Stanford University psychologist Carol Dweck. It provides decades' worth of research on how powerful our minds truly are and what separates those who achieve greatness from those who don't. It has nothing to do with talent. I encourage everyone to read this book; rediscover the power of your mind and make it work to your advantage.

5. Discover the incredible benefits of meditation. In my own personal experience, especially when the going gets tough or I seem to be in a rut, meditation has been one of the best ways to shift my body and mind to happiness and success. Numerous specialists and spiritualists provide online podcasts and classes on meditation and contemplation exercises. I have also benefited greatly from a top-rated app on my smartphone called Calm. It will immerse you in scenes of natural beauty and soothe your mind with relaxing music and nature sounds. Calm also provides fifty guided meditations to assist you with building your self-confidence and creativity.

THINGS YOU CAN TACKLE NOW TO REPROGRAM YOUR BODY

Being a former athlete, I've always made working out and taking care of my body an integral part of my life. I first noticed the importance of working out and staying in tip-top shape when I got hurt in San Diego and I received an injury settlement from the Chicago Bears. As I mentioned earlier, this was one of the few times in my life when I was so depressed I didn't want anyone to see me out in public. I wasn't exercising due to my injury, so I didn't work on my lower body for quite some time. I just wallowed around in bed in self-pity. But I didn't feel good physically, let alone mentally or emotionally. So one day, I decided to get out of the house and go to the gym. I couldn't believe how good it felt to be physical again. The workout transformed my views about my situation.

A miracle didn't happen the exact moment I worked out, but it reminded me of the incredible benefits of optimal fitness. Athletes are programmed to work out for so long that it becomes a part of who they are. Then as life goes on, and especially for the athletes who retire or don't play their specific sports anymore, they forget how important it is to make fitness an ongoing priority.

Sure, it's easy to get lazy and not go to the gym when you're going through a difficult time. I've been there before. I feel we are all in that spot at one time or another. But I know that one thing you can't afford to do is slack off on your health and fitness. This is crucial when it comes to reprogramming your life.

1. Stay active. You have two choices right now: Continue to feel sorry for yourself for all the mishaps and failures you've encountered, or stand up for your life and continually move forward. The key to moving forward, even if you don't know how, is to stay active! So many people stop going out there and experiencing new things. They stop taking care of their bodies and eating healthy foods. Just get going. "Just Do It," as Nike says. Even a ten-minute walk will help you move in the right direction. There have been countless times when I was frustrated or feeling really down, and I went for a short run and felt wonderful afterward. You may wonder how going to the gym for a good workout or eating healthy foods can help turn failure into a gift. Or, for that matter, how it helps you achieve more. Well, no, working out will not automatically turn failure into a gift, but it sets up a physiological state in your body that helps you think better and function more positively. An accumulation of the right things will absolutely enable you to turn failure into a gift—into a winning play.

2. Experiment. As time progressed, I continued to experiment with how my mind and outlook changed after I worked out and started to eat healthy foods again. It was fascinating. I felt like a scientist investigating my mental and physical state. I viewed myself as a computer programmer who was continually tweaking my software programs and reprogramming my data. I experimented with different foods, too, and I noticed how sugar would give me a high, but then I'd plummet a little bit later on. I learned that sugar is a drug. This led me to dig a little deeper and examine different studies and research foods on how they affect our health, including our mental and emotional states. Then I studied the psychological and physiological advantages working out gives us.

3. Fight the trap. Don't let yourself fall into a trap of working so fixedly on a project or job that you let exercise take second place. I have always been extremely active, so it was really hard for me when I decided to stop being a professional athlete and playing football. Now I was in a totally different setting where I was flying from airport to airport or sitting down for hours at a time in front of a computer screen. Even for this book, I dedicated entire days at a time to writing. There would be times when I couldn't think straight anymore, or it was difficult to get words from my head to the computer. The first thing I would do was go for a run or to the gym for a rigorous workout. An hour later, I would feel wonderful as the dopamine and endorphins regenerated my mind and gave me new energy to go back to the computer and get the job done.

4. Eat to win. The "eat to win" mentality is imperative when you're reprogramming yourself. When you think about it, the old saying "You are what you eat" is absolutely correct. What we put into our bodies greatly affects our focus, energy, and well-being. A junk food diet will lead to a junk performance. I'm sure that some people have the physiological makeup to get away with eating junk...for a while. But eventually, it will take a toll on the body. When we start our morning by consuming healthy foods, we instantly set ourselves up for a productive day.

5. Drink up! It's a natural tendency to look for instant pick-me-ups—I think that's why there are many sugar addicts—but these methods of energy are very short-lived. Instead of rushing to grab a cup of coffee every time you feel sluggish or tired, drink some water. (Trust me, I often go for the coffee, too, but I know better.) The human body is made up of over 70 percent water, and more times than not, when you're feeling sluggish or tired, you are dehydrated. Our bodies need proper hydration to perform at our absolute best. Water contributes to high performance, and that contributes to successfully reprogramming your body and life.

6. Form an accountability partnership. If you find an accountability partner—a spouse, a friend, or a personal trainer—you are setting yourself up for success. Sometimes the last thing we want to do after a long day of juggling professional and personal obligations is to go to the gym. There are times when I don't feel like working out early in the morning, especially if I've stayed up late working the night before. But when I have an accountability partner I can count on to be in my ear, shouting, "One more rep, Matt, one more rep," and then yelling at me if I don't follow through, it pushes me that much more. My friend Mike Neal, linebacker for the Green Bay Packers, was always an accountability partner for me, and he pushed me in the gym. He'd say, "C'mon, meathead, is that all you've got?" And the more he pushed, the better I got.

The next time you feel down, experience a failure, or slump into a funk, get a good workout at the gym, or go for a fast walk or a run. It can't hurt, and you never know, it may just change your entire life. One thing for sure is that it's going to contribute to the overall reprogramming of your life.

E *Stands for "Extraordinary"*

The last letter in FAILURE is *E*, which stands for "extraordinary." You've been working through all the letters in the acronym, culminating in an extraordinary you. You are a divine spark of an *extraordinary* God, and in case no one has ever told you, you were put here on earth to do *extraordinary* things and make an *extraordinary* difference in the world. Quite a lofty mission, isn't it?

When most people come face-to-face with failure, they forget their personal power and how extraordinary they really are. I can guarantee that you will get knocked down in life and experience failures of all different shapes and sizes. You will lose loved ones, and your heart and spirit will be crushed. You will fall short of achieving goals from time to time. That's life.

We often lose interest in ourselves and our lives, especially after a hardship, tragedy, or failure. We get trapped in a rut and simply forget who we are. We tell ourselves that our dreams don't matter or that they're impossible. We become depressed, lethargic, negative, and sometimes even ill. But when we do this, we're forgetting our divine birthright. And why would we want to do that?

I have thought about death before, contemplated my self-worth, and wondered, *Why is Matt Mayberry even alive?* The most important thing to remember is that failures and hardships are part of a proven process to shape you into becoming the extraordinary person you were created to be. For the majority of my life, I didn't know how powerful and extraordinary I really was, but realizing that truth changed my life completely.

I had plenty of support and unconditional love from my family members and friends, especially my parents, Grampa Dee, and Coach Hep, who showed me how to acknowledge the extraordinary qualities within me. This helped develop my strengths and birth my own reawakening, which led to a complete reprogramming of my entire life.

TACKLE THIS TODAY

If you find yourself without the loving support from family, friends, or mentors, find groups of people whom you can trust. Unite with the best of the best. Seek out mentors, teachers, coaches, and leaders who are willing to provide a support system for you. Everyone needs someone in their corner, someone who will push them and help them become the extraordinary individual they are.

I know not everyone has the love and support from family members, coaches, and friends, like I've been blessed with. But don't let that diminish your personal power or chances of becoming great and achieving your goals. It just means that you need to look for—and unite with—a circle of trusted friends, peers, and mentors who will be there for you and help you become all you're destined to be.

If you let your imagination go crazy for a moment, let yourself feel what it would be like to accomplish a secret dream of yours. Maybe you'd like to learn how to play guitar. Maybe you'd prefer to paint a picture. Or maybe you'd rather try skydiving. What if you knew you couldn't fail? It's an exhilarating thought, isn't it? When you draw from your personal power and utilize all the letters in the FAILURE acronym, you build self-confidence to tackle anything you want to do.

Most people never realize the extraordinary potential within them because they don't try. Some of the most talented people in the world never get their idea off the ground, never write the book they've always wanted to write, never start their own business, or never do anything remarkable. And it was all because of fear, doubt, negativity, fear, and Mr. Decrease. Remember how important it is to increase your mind, body, intellect, and strength? That's because you want to kick Mr. Decrease to the curb. He's the antithesis of extraordinary.

I always established enormous goals, but when the going got rough, I'd stop and think, *I must be kidding myself. I can't do that.* It's a natural human reaction when negative thoughts start bombarding you. Give them a good kick in the butt and get on with your life.

There is a huge difference between *feeling* fear and *allowing* that fear to hold you back. Fear can help you in many situations. It can alert you to dangerous situations; it can caution you to use common sense. It can be used in a positive way. But you have to be careful and not let it override your positivity. Fear wants you to stall and stay still. Fear and mediocrity go hand in hand. Don't let them defeat you like they have defeated so many. We have to move past the fear and take action to achieve goals.

If you line up some of the best innovators, thought leaders, and extreme achievers, I can almost guarantee you that they will tell you they were afraid when they first took action on their ideas. They were not all that confident whether the idea was brilliant. But they didn't stop. They didn't let the fear or the thought of failure derail them.

THINGS YOU CAN TACKLE NOW TO
BECOME EVEN MORE EXTRAORDINARY

I challenge you from here on out to constantly expand your vision regarding the possibilities in your life. Use faith as the backbone to build your life. Trust that there's something bigger than yourself. Trust that you were born to be more than you ever dreamed possible.

1. Vision. See yourself as extraordinary, a champion, a victor. Practice "visioning" this every day. The more you envision this, the more realistic and tangible your vision becomes in your mind.

2. One-day contract. Draft a contract with yourself just for today. This contract commits you to "Get Better Today," as Coach Hep professed. It outlines specific things you can do to improve yourself and increase in all areas of your life. A good book to read that explores this concept further is *The One-Day Contract: How to Add Value to Every Minute of Your Life* by Rick Pitino, head basketball coach at the University of Louisville. In the book, he describes the one-day contract he created for himself and his team before the start of their championship season in 2013. I've been doing something similar in my own life for the past five years, and it's a great tool. Here's an example:

(Today's date)
I, Matt Mayberry, abide by the terms of this contract. I commit to doing the best I can today in all areas of my

life. I commit to uplifting and encouraging everyone I encounter. I commit to spending my time wisely, prioritizing my responsibilities, and directing all my focus and energy on my most important tasks. I commit to doing all I can do to complete everything that's on my to-do list for today. I commit to being passionate about everything I do. I commit to learning something new today. Just for now, I will GBT, and I will be extraordinary.

3. The illusion of security. No matter if you work in a corporate environment, the government, or the military, or even if you're self-employed, there's really no such thing as job security. Oftentimes, though, people will be lulled into a sense of complacency. It's easy in a corporate environment where one is guaranteed a salary, health insurance, and vacation and sick pay. But when you become too complacent, you can lose sight of your goals and dreams.

4. Be adaptable. Many people are resistant to change. They don't know how to adapt to something new, or they're afraid of trying. In order to reprogram yourself, you need to be flexible and adapt if necessary. That may mean you'll have to go back to school, move to another city, develop a new skill, or intern at a company to see if you like the work and culture.

5. Know your worth. When you truly understand how extraordinary you really are, there's no way you'll let a failure or hardship derail you. Sure, you may get discouraged and upset, and you may even lose some of your self-confidence. But those things are short-lived. People who are extraordinary may cry one day, but the next day they pick themselves up and soldier on. They reprogram themselves so they won't ever have to go through that experience again. It's because they know how valuable they are. They know they're meant for greatness and that they're a spark of God. Nothing can extinguish their bright light. Look at yourself. Do you know how valuable, how beautiful, you are?

———————————

As I come to the close of my story, I want to remind each and every one of you that you carry an amazing capacity for being magnificent. For excelling beyond your wildest dreams. For being extraordinary.

Don't worry. I'll be back. But I must leave you for now. It's time to go to the gym and work out, where I'll continually say to myself, "Get Better Today." I'll smile because I know Coach Hep is watching over me. I'll hear Grampa Dee telling me, "Matt, you are special. You are going to do something great with your life." I'll embrace his encouragement, support, and love in every set of reps I do. And in every dream and goal I set out to achieve. No matter what I do or where I go, I'll leave the door open just a bit…a tiny bit…so the light can get in.

Remember, we are all the carriers of our stories and our dreams. We are the architects of our lives, and we can reclaim, renew, and reprogram ourselves for success starting now. We have a beautiful life waiting for us just beyond the meadow. Can you see it? Out there is where the dreams are waiting.

ACKNOWLEDGMENTS

Books have the potential to change and transform lives. When I was at the lowest and darkest moments of my life, it was the books I read that would eventually change my life forever. I had a dream for this book for a long time, and the only reason you have it in your hands right now is because of the incredible contributions of so many people.

I would like to thank...

Center Street, for giving me the opportunity to bring this book to life and work tirelessly to refine the manuscript. To the Center Street team—Kate Hartson, Alexa Smail, Grace Tweedy, Katie Broaddus, Rolf Zettersten, Carolyn Kurek, Andrea Glickson, Pasty Jones, and Katie Connors: Thank you for making me better and for challenging me along the way.

The best agent in the entire world, Katie Kotchman. I know every author talks about how awesome their agent is, but I truly believe that my agent is one of a kind. She not only challenges me every day to become a better writer, but she also acts as a trusted adviser. Katie, this book wouldn't be possible without your relentless help.

Donna Peerce, for being available at all times of the day to hear my crazy ideas and do everything in your power to help bring my dreams to fruition. Donna, you are more than just a book doctor. You are a friend and someone I deeply admire. None of this would be possible without your effort and willingness to put up with me.

Xaviera, for your never-ending love and support. You believed in me when at times I didn't even fully believe in myself. You have been an enormous blessing in my life.

My incredible mentors Matthew Kelly, A. C. McLean, and Jon Gordon for your time and energy in helping me out early on. I had a message to share but was completely lost on how to go about sharing it. Thank you for your counsel and for pointing me in the right direction.

My biggest supporters through it all, my parents. I wouldn't be where I am today without the best two parents in the world. You have never missed a sporting event in my entire life and have given endless sacrifices to see me succeed professionally. I am forever indebted to you.

The staff and former teammates at Indiana University and Hinsdale South High School who were a part of my journey. This is your book just as much as it is mine.

SUGGESTED READING LIST

Mindset: The New Psychology of Success, by Carol Dweck

The Magic of Thinking Big, by David J. Schwartz

Failing Forward: Turning Mistakes into Stepping Stones for Success, by John C. Maxwell

Intentional Living: Choosing a Life That Matters, by John C. Maxwell

How Successful People Grow, by John C. Maxwell

The Energy Bus: 10 Rules to Fuel Your Life, Work, and Team with Positive Energy, by Jon Gordon

The Rhythm of Life: Living Every Day with Passion and Purpose, by Matthew Kelly

Think and Grow Rich, by Napoleon Hill

The Power of Positive Thinking, by Norman Vincent Peale

The One-Day Contract: How to Add Value to Every Minute of Your Life, by Rick Pitino

Identity: Your Passport to Success, by Stedman Graham

Awaken the Giant Within: How to Take Immediate Control of Your Mental, Emotional, Physical, and Financial Destiny, by Tony Robbins

See You at the Top, by Zig Ziglar

ABOUT THE AUTHOR

Matt Mayberry, a former NFL linebacker for the Chicago Bears, is the CEO of Matt Mayberry Enterprises. One of the most widely read columnists for *Entrepreneur* magazine, Matt is an acclaimed keynote speaker, thought leader, and maximum performance strategist. Matt specializes in helping maximize the performance of individuals and organizations all over the world.

Matt is Indiana University's current record holder for most sacks in a single game, and he was the team recipient for the prestigious Howard Brown Award, which exemplifies leadership, courage, and work ethic. With a 4.45 forty-yard dash, Mayberry was signed by the Chicago Bears in 2010. Reaching the pinnacle of his sport, he suffered a life-changing injury. It was this event that inspired Mayberry to embrace his true passion—his true gift—helping others achieve success. Once the glory of his NFL dreams had faded, Matt Mayberry discovered his mission in life and is passionately enjoying every aspect.

Now, as a sensitive and self-aware facilitator, Matt sees the potential for growth in others and devotes his energy to help businesses and individuals achieve it. Moreover, as an engaging, natural motivator, Matt inspires others toward